Viral Marketing

Building Buzz and Getting Your
Dream Clients

*(Use the Power of Video and Virality to Grow Your
Online Brand)*

Gary Woodall

Published By **Jordan Levy**

Gary Woodall

All Rights Reserved

Viral Marketing: Building Buzz and Getting Your Dream Clients (Use the Power of Video and Virality to Grow Your Online Brand)

ISBN 978-1-7780579-9-1

No part of this guidebook shall be reproduced in any form without permission in writing from the publisher except in the case of brief quotations embodied in critical articles or reviews.

Legal & Disclaimer

TABLE OF CONTENTS

Introduction

Let's make one thing plain: a lot of people attempt "viral marketing" but fail. The reason should be clear. Most people aren't aware of the concept behind viral marketing. about. In fact the more they hear about the term and hear about it, the more confused they are. It increases the likelihood that they will get burned and fall over every time they try "viral advertising."

Let me clue you in to the hidden technique. The secret to viral marketing lies about joining a specific group of people.

You wouldn't believe it, those who are interested by what it is that you're advertising are already forming on the internet. Maybe they have a well-known Twitter profile. Perhaps they've joined many different Facebook groups and pages. Many of them are dedicated to this particular audience.

A majority of people who are trying to make use of viral marketing aren't aware of this. They aren't aware the fact that this niche marketing channel currently exists.

What's the secret? It's as simple as signing up to the correct network and then'resharing content that has already become viral. Here it is. The cat has escaped from the bag.

A lot of people fall short with this type of marketing due to the belief they have to develop their own concepts. What they really want to do is to reinvent the wheel. Why should you gamble using content that is likely to not going anywhere? Instead, focus on what's already well-known to your viewers.

Then choose something that is highly sought-after on Twitter and then reshare it on Facebook along with several other Twitter accounts, which may not have seen the content that's viral you're sharing. Make use of the diverse social media platforms' tag systems as well as other ways to recognize your audience.

YouTube Twitter, YouTube, Facebook along with other popular social media sites are eager to see you succeed. They want your content to be a success. Why? The more well-known your website's content becomes the more attention they will receive.

It's beneficial that you have access to the tools that will help you market your content. The more prominent you become more likely you'll attract new people to their platform. This is why every one of these networks has its individual tagging systems and ways to increase visibility. Use these methods. Get visitors from them. Then, redirect all the traffic on your website.

What is the best way you are going to convince people? Perhaps you can test presenting an ad to them. If you place the right advert in front of the correct eyes, you could get many clicks. Some of these clicks could turn into hard cold dollars.

You should make the majority of your visitors into mailing list subscribers in the best way you are able to. It is also possible to ask your readers to visit to your blog and if they are interested in the content, sign up to join your mailing list. If you've got lots of people on your mailing list , and they're truly committed to your blog content, the chances are that you can turn the mailing list into a regular income stream.

This book provides the tips to viral marketing, which allow you to reduce time, cash and avoid unnecessary stress. It's no surprise that if you adhere to the guidelines I give throughout this guide, you will increase the chances of succeeding by utilizing viral marketing.

Chapter 1: You're Not Subject To Be A Viral Marketing Failing

Don't be a part of the group of Viral Content Failures

The essence in viral advertising is the content. In simple terms, you must to find content that is viral so you can draw large amounts of traffic from various websites on the internet and turn this traffic into profit.

The problem is, it's easy to fail in producing "viral" material. It's true.

Many marketers are of the belief that if they "create it, they're going to be there." Sorry, but publishing "hot extraordinary or original material" on your site will not suffice. The posting of great content is not enough to create a viral effect.

It's a lot of money to create original content. You probably know this firsthand. Maybe you tried hiring someone to write the material for you. Perhaps you attempted creating it yourself.

No matter how hard you tried to do it, the concept is the same. It's pricey. You can make payment in cash or the way of time.

Viral Success Everything Comes Down to the correct eyeballs

In simple terms, you need to attract visitors from a niche. The secret to viral marketing isn't huge quantities of views. It's not an utterly overwhelming amount of traffic. In reality the organic view or visibility does not translate into a lot of money. Really.

Millions of views will not generate any real income unless the views come from the right viewers. If you're trying to earn money from YouTube videos, and you make dollars per 1,000 views and traffic, in itself isn't enough to pay for your bills.

Viral Content Pieces aren't Commodities

I'm sure I've informed you that one of the key elements of viral marketing success is to identify items that have gained the attention of Facebook and then share it on Twitter as well as YouTube. But there's an limit.

It is important to note that even if it's popular on Twitter however, that doesn't necessarily suggest that it's going to get the same amount of attention with Pinterest, Facebook or Instagram. Additionally, if you're sharing videos it's difficult to do the same thing on Pinterest. Pinterest is a site that is geared to images.

Although you may get quite a bit of traffic, remember the fact that this isn't as simple as just moving content from one site to another.

It doesn't matter how popular a viral post.

I'm sure you're amazed. You're probably thinking "Are you insane? Are you trying to tell me that even if my blog post gets tons of likes, comments , and favorite posts, my content is poor?" That's exactly what I'm trying to say.

The measurements aren't making an impact. What is the thing that can make a difference? Retweets and shares. These are the only actions that have a positive impact as they play a key part in determining the amount and how often your content is distributed across the globe.

It's not really a matter of concern that you own an article that receives a lot of comments and is awash with favorite and likes. It won't help you. You need the right eyeballs.

When you consider the fact that people who follow others or have friends tend to share the same desires, it makes sense to have your content distributed as widely as is possible. If people share your content on Facebook most likely, they will send it to people who have the same interest in your niche. This is what you should be striving at.

I've found a number of hidden secrets in this chapter. Be aware that it's not about the information. Instead, it's about right attention. It's not possible to treat viral content as if it were some sort of product. Additionally, the vast majority of social indicators do not really play a role in viral marketing.

Chapter 2: Can Find Viral Content Anywhere
Viral Content Is All Around!

It's true that there are a lot of things that go viral in Twitter and Facebook every single day. According to an estimate that is relatively recent of over 2 million fresh pieces of content are posted every single day. It is likely that there's a lot of is shared on social networks as well as on the internet generally.

Content becomes viral on a regular basis. There are numerous reasons to this. First, the content is likely to have an emotional effect. Perhaps it's funny, perhaps it's stunning, perhaps it angers folks. Whatever the reason is, people get so upset that they don't hesitate to share the content.

Another reason is pure adorableness. If you find yourself constantly watching cute kittens in videos, it is the cute factor at play. It's pretty obvious. This can be the case for infants or animals, as well as older people doing things that are entertaining. If you can find something cute, you can bet that there's a good chance that the piece of content will be shared many times.

Another popular reason for virality is the shock factor. The viewers are often shocked or awed by what takes position in this video. Maybe it's a tale of criminal act. It could be something shocking, scandalous or embarrassing.

People love to see something fresh. People love being thrown off each and every now and then. It's like explaining the appeal of trains wrecks. It's true that you shouldn't be watching these, but people take it on regardless.

Another reason the reason content becomes viral is the simple element of novelty. In the event that there's some sort of breakthrough in science that shocks the world and you are not surprised in the event that it becomes viral.

In addition, the content could become viral if the content mentions to you something that you aren't aware of. You may already be familiar with the information however, it is re-sends the content in an captivating and attractive manner. This type of content is like a kind of brain candy.

These are the types of content that go everywhere, every single day. There's no specific specialization. It's possible that you're watching the latest viral video about something that is usually boring, like furniture however there's something about the video that just grabs your interest. It's hard not to discuss it with your pals.

Psychological Foundation of Content Virality

Let's make it clear that when you share information on your private network, you're making yourself available. The bomb could explode into your face. If you post material that a lot of people do not like it could be a loss of the reputation of your brand. Yet, people are sharing content on Facebook timelines and Twitter feeds frequently.

What is the reason they do this? What can they gain from it? How do they deal with the psychological aspects that are at work?

First of all, people are prone to sharing content as they want to be seen as "hip." They want to be perceived as cool or people who are knowledgeable about the internet. They want to become the very first person to post something interesting that's rapidly becoming popular on the internet. There's a tremendous emotional satisfaction associated with being the first person to share interesting content.

Another reason is to enjoy and exert one's influence. I don't know about others but it makes me feel good whenever I share something that I am interested in or am passionate about, and then my fellow friends also share and reshare the same things.

In essence, they affirm my views whenever I observe that. They inform me, in many different ways that their opinion is important. Every share my content gets is a vote to my own authority, credibility, and credibility.

People post content because they believe it's important or useful. Simply put, it represents the range of interests of individuals.

The key point: if their systems are fine-tuned to the point where they have the same range of interests, it is likely that your content will become viral.

If you're fascinated by rabbits and I am a lover of rabbits, and I post videos of cute rabbits, chances are that you'll be tempted be tempted to hit"share" or click the "share" button when you see my status update to your timeline. Chances are that you have friends with an interest in similar things. There are likely to be friends with an interest in rabbits. They are likely to be sharing your content.

Don't underestimate the importance of how "viral" shared interests could be, since that's how Facebook is designed. When you add someone to your network of friends chances are they're from the same area similar to yours. They've had the same experiences, attended the same school and have an array of shared things to do. These overlapping common interests that give life to the phenomenon of virality.

What is the most honest Truth about viral content marketing?

There are a variety of points you need to get your head around. If you can master this, you are likely to succeed in the world of viral marketing. If you don't do this, you'll be a mess for a long time to come. You're going to struggle.

First of all it's not necessary to come up with something completely unique. Then, you can reuse the work of someone else. In the final instance, you could reverse engineer your rivals' viral media and content. Take all this together and you have everything you need for a successful social media marketing plan that is viral.

Chapter 3: How To Avoid This To Reduce Time And Money

Let's be clear It is possible to create your own personal content and hope that somehow it will go popular. You're certainly welcome to take this route. But let me warn you that, if that is your intention you're likely to lose an enormous amount of time, money, and energy.

I personally find no thing more annoying than putting a lot of effort, time and emotional energy into something without seeing any tangible results: no traffic no sales, and no money. You just need to endure a few additional weeks or days of this experience to decide to stop.

This is precisely why many people do not succeed in viral marketing. They find that it's not working which is why they give up. In reality, they are set to fail. They are disappointed in themselves.

What is the reason? The purpose behind the wrong approach. They attempt to create something new, exciting extraordinary, creative and innovative. But for every marketer who pulls that out, they have many others who fall short.

My Advice to You is not to even try

Let's talk about it. If you believe that a concept for content is popular and " will become viral," it won't always suggest that it's going to. In reality in the majority of cases it doesn't happen.

If you're not able to understand the thinking patterns of your market's members If you are unable to read their minds, you may be better to not create your own content. Making a new, viral content is costly both in terms of cost as well as time.

The Superior Way

What is the best method of performing the viral marketing of content? First of all it is important to concentrate on the area you are in. Be aware that not all of the viral videos that is being repeated over and over are in your field. In actual fact, the majority of them aren't within your field.

Concentrate on the established winners in your niche. It is important to look at the amount instances they've received shares. It is important to look at the amount of times they've been shared on Twitter and retweeted. These are fantastic indicators of how popular they have become.

It's crucial to pay attention to the number of shares that a piece of content has been given. This is a good indicator about the degree to which it is "viral" this content has become.

I'll tell you that it doesn't matter the number of people who like it, share it with friends, comment on it, nothing it makes any difference. If they do this, they're not endorsement of the content with their own ring of influence. They're not promoting that particular piece of content out to other people who have similar desires when they leave comments or click"like" or click the "like" option.

Don't waste your time worrying about indicators of social engagement that do nothing to propel the ball ahead. Take note of what matters. Consider the number of times a piece in content was shared and tweeted or retweeted.

After you've found this material and verified that it is relevant to your area of expertise, you can add an action call to action in order to draw the attention of those who are part of your audience. This is a crucial aspect of the process.

If you're just trying to snare niche content that was previously viral, you're not creating much value. Also, you're creating pipe dreams for yourself.

Why is that? It's likely that the vast majority of people sharing the charming video you found and reshared do not belong to your segment. It is important to prompt people to click an online link that is accompanied by the viral video or picture that screens your targeted viewers.

For example, if you're passing around an audio recording of a cat who is high-fiving the owner, you could make a call to action that reads, "For awesome cat training ideas, visit this website."

Please be aware that the vast majority of people who share this adorable and humorous video of cat giving high-fives are likely not even own cats. They just think that it's hilarious. They simply believe it's amazing and adorable. They believe it puts people's smiles. But let me assure youthat most of them will not be your market.

The best part is, by putting a call to take action on the content you are sharing people who belong to your targeted people will visit your site. They are prequalified. This is the method by which you can piggyback on tried and confirmed viral content that is directly or to a certain degree relevant to your targeted segment.

Chapter 4: Secret To A Successful Viral Marketing

The Secret to Viral Effectiveness Marketing

I know that I've made this point in the last chapter. To bring the message home, I'll fully explain the key steps you have to take to run highly successful campaign for marketing that is viral. These marketing campaigns that are viral will perform their work not just on your social media platforms, but also on your website, in your forum posts, and any other marketing initiatives on the internet.

Step #1: Find What's Hot

The first thing you must do is find out what's most popular on the internet. There are a lot of hyperlinks, images as well as image quotes and videos that are constantly going viral. People can't help but share the content.

Identify Hot Stuff.

When you've stumbled across this content make sure you review them according to how relevant to the niche you are trying to reach. For instance, if promote a plumbing business located in Florida You could share all the funny dogs on scooters you like. There is also the possibility of attracting an abundance of traffic to your website. But, guess what? Most likely, you won't create a large number of appointments for your client using these videos.

There is a chance that you will get a number of eyes however, they're the wrong ones. Why? The videos you shared and promoted aren't relevant enough to the niche you want to target.

Niches are people who have certain problems. They are those looking for specific common solutions. Keep this in your mind. Even if you receive lots of traffic, it's not a guarantee.

Step 2 Step 2: Share viral content with your friends to drive sales

It's crucial to know the reason behind viral marketing at all. This is the place where a lot of people fall down. They really do. Why? They focus on numbers. They focus on getting as many clicks on their website as is possible.

Don't get me wrong. Traffic is fantastic but it has to be the right kind of traffic.

In the event that I were to choose one of 1 million viewers who are casual and 1,000 viewers who are highly targeted I'd choose the latter daily. What's the purpose of having 1 million viewers when only one of a million changes into a paying customer?

Imagine receiving 1,000 viewers who are certified and seeing 200, 300 or 500 turning into actual customers. It's not an unimaginable feat. It should be fairly obvious.

It is important to understand how this operates and be aware of what you should be focused paying attention to. It's not about traffic on the internet. It's about something else. It's all about making sales.

You must get those who are on the right page so they are able to do something that can increase the cash you have into your account. This is the most important thing. It should be your goal.

This is the reason it's essential to share viral content to boost sales. There's no way to drive traffic. just trying to increase visibility, you're trying to increase sales.

How can you achieve this? Make sure you share the blog's content in your website. Re-share the link of your blog via social media. Make use of these to attract people to your site. Then, you can turn this traffic into potential sales by urging the potential customers to sign up to your newsletter.

This is how you win the game. It is possible to convert potential customers via a blog that is built-in. When they click an image and they end into a fascinating web page that they like, they could be enthralled by your blog content to the point that they click the link to be informed about the latest updates. This is the way to lock them into.

You could also offer an offer for free, such as a kind of manual for consumers. For example, if your website offers the legal services for immigration, then you may want to offer an informative brochure for free that informs users on how they can be able to enter the USA using the tourist visa with minimal hassles.

Whatever you do, make sure to get people to sign up to your mailing list because of the fact that once they've signed up, you can send them periodic updates, which could possibly lead them to affiliate products or even get the people to buy your items. The possibilities are endless.

Your email list that does the work of convincing those who subscribe to your list. They may not be interested in reading one update, but should they go through an update and like an article, you can turn that interest into a sale. This is how efficient the subscriber list can be.

Your entire strategy for viral marketing must be focused on bringing conversions into your email newsletter. The more people are subscribed to your newsletter , and the better value of the content the more money you could earn in the end.

Chapter 5: What To Do To Find The Correct Content

Finding Hot Content

Given that you've got an notion of the two-step strategy for a successful viral advertising campaign How do you complete step 1? There are two ways to do it. You can choose to take the more difficult route, or you can opt for the shortcut.

In order to ensure you have an accurate knowledge about the screening procedure involved I'll explain the two options in detail. You can first try to carry out the process by hand. You could get extremely specific material using this labor-intensive method.

The first step you need to do is go to the Google Keyword Planner tool. If you're not certain the meaning of that, log in with Google Ads and click on their tool link. Once you click, you will be shown options that provide an overview of the Google Keyword Planner resource.

Click on the tool. Add a couple of keywords that directly relate to your field. If you keep doing this, you'll discover a lot of keywords related to your niche.

After you have this extensive list, sort the results based on their accuracy or uniqueness to your particular niche. After you've cleaned your list of keywords, use them to Twitter and Facebook to find accounts on social media that focus on the keywords you have identified.

Naturally, you'll consider the social media profiles of people, businesses or firms that are in your area of expertise. It is possible to tell from how they talk about themselves to determine if they belong within your desired niche.

Be sure to keep an eye on these accounts. Following an extensive procedure, you should have a tidy, neat list of social media profiles of your particular niche competitors. They could be located on Instagram, Pinterest, Facebook, Twitter, YouTube, you know it. The more extensive your list the more impressive.

Find and poach your competitors" or Niche Enthusiasts' Viral Content

Keep in mind that when you click to browse the Facebook and Twitter profiles of businesses and individuals within your area, you're likely to discover that there are two types of accounts: competitors and fans. I'm not even going to define competitors because I believe that this definition is obvious.

Fan accounts are private accounts that are set up by individuals who are just emotionally attached to their niche. In the case, for instance, you're advertising online dog training programs it is possible to access a large collection of dog training Social media profiles. After you have a look at their content, you can see that they're not making money from it. They're sharing their enthusiasm or passions. They're fan accounts. It is recommended to create the entire list too.

After you have compiled an extensive list of niche-specific social media profiles examine all their contents. Take note of the amount of instances their posts have been shared or retweeted. Note down photos or videos, interesting images, links or any other type of media.

You can be able to see, this process isn't easy. It is essential to comprehend the process. You must know what you are looking for. Additionally, you need lots of time. If you work hard, it can burn the entire day.

The Faster Method: Buzzsumo.com

If you don't have the time or patience to search for all your niche competitors as well as niche followers' social media accounts and utilize their content, use BuzzSumo. The online platform is designed to search through the main social media platforms to find content relevant to your specific keywords.

Make sure you make sure to save the niche keywords you have gotten from Google Keyword Planner tool and use the keywords on BuzzSumo. There will be lots of content that has been easily filtered by certain indicators of social media like retweets or shares. BuzzSumo is a great tool because it can save you an incredible number of hours, effort and frustration.

Find Your Links All Set

Once you've reviewed your competition's most popular pieces of content, copy the URLs of those sites and paste them on an Excel spreadsheet. On the right you will find the description of that piece of content. Usually when you come across the most popular content on a social media platform it will have a short description, or perhaps an article headline. Utilize these resources.

Chapter 6: Tips To Optimizely Find Your Niche With The Correct Content

How do you treat it?

If you've compiled your reverse-engineered material, remember that you are using them to build trust on your social media profiles and eventually bring traffic to your website. Your website of choice could be an actual site, or it could be an article collection websites, or could be a blog.

Whatever way you decide to setup it the way you do it, you'll be using third-party content to build your brand's reputation and to build their following. What will draw people from these accounts to your web pages, target sites or sites that are material or adverts that you are able to revolve around the curated content.

I hope this is obvious to you. You'll be posting content from third parties that you have curated to your social networks account. You may be thinking, "Isn't this prohibited? Shouldn't they raise some objection?" They shouldn't.

It's a win-win situation. Your site is driving visitors to their pages while creating your own authority in the niche. Additionally, you're inviting people to take action by encouraging them to share your page with friends or join you on Instagram as well as Twitter or whatever other social media platforms you're using.

It's a win-win situation. The people who curate the content will benefit from publicity and traffic for their brand. You, meanwhile, get to develop your social media accounts.

When you've built up an extensive audience, a greater number of people will view the direct hyperlinks to your sales pages. They will click on the link and get additional visitors to your email-squeeze page. This can result in an increased email list which can lead to a variety of revenue-generating possibilities in the future. This is how you make money. All it boils all the way to reverse engineering, and curating other's content.

Improved Curated Content

I would like to tell you that you're able to take any third-party viral content and market them in the same way. That's exactly what others are doing. Unfortunately, if you do manage to achieve this, you'll be leaving money in the sand.

It's important to realize that you're not merely trying to increase traffic through carefully curated content. This shouldn't be your main goal. The primary goal of your business is not to increase traffic. Instead, your main goal is to draw in niche-targeted people to view your content.

The more people you contact you can increase the likelihood that they will click that link on your media account and become a page liker or follower or fan of your channel. Whatever shape it takes the goal is to get a huge amount of people who follow your account. You're trying to build an audience.

It will be difficult to do this if you're disseminating curated content using the same titles that were first used. Some people might notice that your content isn't authentically original, and they are likely to dismiss it. In addition, the content is popular, so they may seen it before from some other source.

The first step you should take after you've screened your the content you have curated for uniqueness is to modify the headlines. Develop titles that are targeted to your niche for all the content you've curated. Make sure to emphasize the importance of the content.

For instance, if you run a dropshipping business that sells cat pendants, and you've come across excellent viral videos featuring adorable kittens, make sure you include the name of your videos in the description. draws people in or informs them about your product.

It's not an easy task as you have to present it in a captivating manner However, if you can give it enough time, you can create a great specific name that will make people excited with your specific niche social media page.

Create Niche-Targeted Descriptions and Commentary for Curated Content

Not only should you rewrite the name of the item which you're poaching you must also duplicate the same for the description or commentary.

It's essential to make the obvious that the content was designed to appeal to an audience that is specific to. So that when the material is released, it makes it's way across the web and all social media platforms it will be able to filter users who might be interested in the information. Only those who truly interested in your area would be able to go to the page you have incorporated into the content in order to return to your social media account.

Utilize Niche-Targeted Hashtags

This tip pertains to people who are using the curated content feature for their accounts on Instagram or Twitter. If you've completed the right research at Chapter 4 or 5, you should be aware of Twitter hashtags that are well-known in your particular field.

Create a list of them. Use them when you share content that you have curated via Twitter as well as Instagram. This way it allows you to "piggyback" with hashtags that are looked up by those who are interested in your particular niche. This is how you can get targeted attention.

In the end, the goal is not to attract a bunch of mostly uninterested people to your social media pages. You're actually trying to attract a large number of people who are attracted to your particular area and, in turn, get them to join your social media.

Don't overlook the secondary impacts of Viral Content Curated

Viral content is extremely effective because it doesn't just attract people who are already interested in your field, but also get users to share your content with their own social networks. This could lead others with similar interests, or even similar interests, to look up the hyperlinks for your respective social media profiles.

Be aware of the way this second traffic impact plays out in the creation of titles, commentary and descriptions. You're not simply repackaging the latest content. You're trying to reach people and their friends as well as their friends who share similar niche interests.

I want to give an overview of this to help you understand the significance of this. It's not something that you can just browse through. You must put the right attention in order to get the most benefit from the ability to target your audience with the viral content that you share.

Chapter 7: Do Not Forget To Use Certain Precautions When Sharing The Content Of Others

Be aware of your own safety when sharing content from others

I would like to inform you that you could completely reuse the material of everyone without any legal issues. Naturally that is not the case. If I said this to you then I would be lying.

If you intend to curate tested and proven viral content You must legally safeguard yourself. What can you do to achieve this?

The potential of the CTTO

What exactly does CTTO mean? It is a reference to 'Credit To the Owner.' If you share this, you're declaring to the public that you don't have the content, and you acknowledge ownership to the person who actually owns the content. Be aware that when people post CTTO it is not just a matter of perform it on the spur of the moment.

If you do this successfully will connect to the source. For example, if you post a funny cat video, and it appears like it was that was first popularized by someone who had an account with a personal one, you can include the link to their personal account in your post curated by. Create CTTO and then include the link to that person.

In this way, the public will be able to see that the individual is the owner of the material. This is simply curating the information. This is a crucial element of obtaining legal protection. It is essential to provide an appropriate acknowledgement. You cannot make it appear as if you created this content by yourself.

Make sure to comment on the Content

Within US copyright law , as well as Canadian intellectual property laws, in the event you make use of secured intellectual properties, you could receive some form of protection from lawsuits if you carry out certain actions. The first thing to remember is that your sharing of the content should include some sort of comment. It doesn't matter if you're sharing it to give an original reason or sharing it to promote debate.

This is what the fair usage doctrine operates. It's about finding copyright law in order to facilitate genuine debate. In doing so, every time you make a comment, you are engaging in the fair use doctrine. It's not my intention to suggest that your comments should be brief and simple. It's not likely help you.

If you are curating viral content, your comments should be an original piece of content of it's own. It should be useful. It should produce some sort of impact and, in reality, add something of value for the material you curate. It's not enough to tell people, "Take a look at this" or "Haha funny." This isn't going to accomplish the job.

Take advantage of this amazing opportunity to speak about your topic. Make use of this opportunity to highlight your expertise and authority in your field. In doing so you can get two birds in one stone. Additionally, you are able to are able to qualify your curated content under the fair use principle. This makes it more difficult for the owner of the content to bring actions in court against your in case of copyright violation.

Remember that within the international law of intellectual property, the only person that can distribute copies of their source work would be the creator. Furthermore, that person can assign these rights to an individual. They are the only people that have legal rights in copyright law.

Fair use law provides exceptions in specific contexts regarding the protection. This way you can freely publish content of others, provided that you include comments, or providing value, or arranging it to stimulate conversations.

It is equally important to make sure that the content that you share isn't the complete content. For instance, you're likely to run into trouble when you share a full film that somebody else made. But, if you only provide a portion of the images or videos like the items you can see on Buzzfeed It is likely that you will be okay.

You must determine the amount of content you're sampling or quoting. If you are using all of the content, you could be in trouble. It is essential to link back with the original source. This way the source will benefit from your curating. This is a win-win situation.

In many cases, third party creators of content really don't care. Actually, they'd be happy to help you. Why is that? The more you share their content, the more visitors they get. The more you spread its content the more successful their brand will become. You're doing them a massive favor. The situation can get a little complicated when you share bits of popular television shows. This is when things can become a little tense.

Do yourself a favor and make sure there is a comment alongside the material you're collecting. Be sure to use the term CTTO to ensure your safety. If you also receive any kind of notice or complaint from the rights holder You should take the content that you curated off the site. It's just not worth the effort. You don't want to mess with all the cash you've accumulated and create your own distinctive online identity because you're not willing to give up on the content you have curated.

If you're doing it correctly, you'll have a lot of carefully well-curated content in all cases. It's not much in the event that the rights holder informs you to remove some of the posts you have posted to your personal social media profiles. If you are notified of such a request be sure to act upon them promptly. Do not put off responding to them. You'll end up making it harder for you in the event that they make a an effort to file a lawsuit against you.

No doubt, intellectual property law is very serious. There are penalties are possible to face and may even end up in jail. The consequences could be severe and you should be sure to do yourself a big favor and make sure you are secure in sharing other people's content.

It is important to understand that what makes this difficult to understand is that once content is viral on the internet the content is typically changed hands multiple times. In reality the possibility is that this has happened enough that you do not know who the real person who owns the content is. You don't know who created the content initially.

Do yourself a favor and ensure that you adhere to the above guidelines and are open to receiving down any notifications or alerts.

Chapter 8: Share Viral Content Via Facebook

How can You share viral content on Facebook

You have an excellent understanding of the best method to share viral content and utilizing content curation to grow your blog's social networks and following, here's an entire chapter about viral content marketing on Facebook.

Create Viral Content First on Your Facebook Page

The first thing you'll need to do is to post the curate content on your page on Facebook. This is the first step from which you'll post your posts. Then, you click on the URL for the posted post and then republish additional sections to Facebook as well as Twitter as well as other media platforms using tools like HootSuite.

This handy tool allows you to upload a huge amount in content onto your accounts on social networks, and extend the publication of the content. It also lets you explore the use of hashtags, comments and headlines. The great thing is that HootSuite is that you don't have to monitor the accounts on social networks by telling it what time it is to publish.

It is enough to set the time and get the application and then forget about it. Once you've completed all of your content you're able to sit in and relax and let HootSuite perform its job. If people check your social media profiles they will see that you're operating your account as you're posting on a regular basis.

What they aren't aware of is that you've indeed set up this system in advance and it was your software that published this content. This is a great method to streamline your process so that you don't have to be physically or personally doing the job. Many people earn a great passive income simply by using tools like HootSuite to post edited content to their social media pages.

They then direct visitors towards their email lists. The lists are created to provide special offers at specific time periods. The users and owners of these systems relax and build up cash. Yes, it's to be quite impressive however, you must be able to have an effective system and an unmistakable plan of action if you are planning to achieve this.

When should you republish?

If you've done your research correctly You should have plenty of viral content within your field. This is an art. These types of content are acknowledged to attract an impressive amount of attention within your particular field. The problem is, you shouldn't be publishing the same content over and over.

In the case, for instance, if you have 300 links , and you've put together HootSuite to tweet your content at a frequency of 6 times a day, that means you will have to wait 50 days your listing will be reposted again. You may want to tweet more frequently like 12 times per day, and this will reduce the time frame for reposting by 25 days.

Do you see the problem there? It's likely that you'll lose followers if it comes in their eyes that you're just reusing the same material over and over again. This is why I advise you to acquire a significant amount of content to ensure that even if you're posting at a frequent frequency each day the reposting will not be evident.

Then why Bother Reposting?

It is possible to accomplish this by tackling them the hard way. You can get an immense collection of content. Then, you can create a system to make sure you're not going to publish the same content multiple times. You're welcome to do so. It takes a lot of effort, time and energy. Many people do not take things this way. Instead, they prefer to share.

If you've got sufficient material that you can reuse, you'll be safe. If you're going be republishing once each two months you is a good idea. Yet, why do you do this? If you can do this, you'll get many parts in the pie. There is a reason why your initial post didn't get your followers' attention but it occurs occasionally. If you do republish the post, you have another chance.

Additionally, when content that is viral becomes popular, it can become extremely cold However, this doesn't mean that people who initially were interested in it have completely lost curiosity. If you post it in the future it could spark curiosity. People might think it's a great throwback, and may share it. This can bring new followers.

If enough time has passed since the initial posting of edited content, you are providing your followers with the impression that they have discovered new content. This is always beneficial.

Always include a link to your Landing Page Using Your Own Curated Viral Content

Every time you share the content that you have curated, virally and you connect to the source. you should give the appropriate acknowledgement, however, you need be sure to hyperlink to your conversion site. It's your email list. If you aren't able to do that then Facebook will post your edited content as that is posted on Facebook. Facebook page.

It could be enough. If you're sharing your direct posts via your facebook page to related Facebook groups, or to other pages, people can choose to like your page and maybe receive updates.

Post your Facebook pages URLs to Niche-related Facebook Groups

Once you've posted several posts for your facebook page. Take the link of the posts and distribute them to Facebook groups with the same area. Be aware that you are not able to do this in the first few days. It is not possible to join an organization and then start sharing hyperlinks. You'll look like an unprofessional spammer. People won't be impressed by the way you're going about it.

Most likely, you're going be banned earlier than later. I would advise against try to get banned.

Instead, join these niche-specific Facebook groups and connect with the members. Ask lots of questions, inform them of your knowledge and appear as a reputable member within the community.

Remember, Facebook groups are nothing more than online message boards. They're like tiny online communities. When you join these communities, behave as a trustworthy community member. Contribute value to discussions through your postings. This is the method through how you establish credibility.

Once you've established credibility and trustworthiness You will then be able to share a part of your content, along with the links to third-party sites that you are sharing. It is important to use this method to cover your areas of concern. It isn't a good idea to be apprehensive in relation to this. People will quickly realize that you're merely marketing your page on Facebook. People aren't happy about the fact that you are doing this. It's just a matter of the time before they decide to are able to ban you.

If you're planning on dropping links, just a small part of it should be on your Facebook page, but the vast majority needs be top-quality content. This is a great way to encourage discussions.

This is how you establish credibility and are allowed to keep publishing your own material. You must build a reputation by establishing yourself as a credible first.

Facebook Viral Content Method

In case I'm not being clear enough. Let me explain it. For Facebook your method of creating viral content must begin by posting your carefully content that you have curated through the Facebook page. Then, you promote your content with related groups to your niche. This will increase the number of likes on your page's Facebook profile. You would like Facebook users to be at your site.

With plenty of details, a certain percentage of your customers may enjoy the page. This indicates that whenever you make updates, specific percentage of your viewers might be able to notice your posts. This can lead to the people who are interested in your links to your sales pages and eventually landing on your website or on your squeeze page.

Then, you can auto-publish your content on your Facebook page in order to get the most of attention on the sales pages. Simply put, continue posting regularly on the Facebook pages you have. Don't be embarrassed about it. It's true that only a small percentage of your Facebook followers will take note of your updates.

The majority of people that have liked the page aren't likely to be able to see your updates unless they select "see first" when they first liked your page. However, generally speaking, only small percentage of your page's fans likely to check your posts which is why it's important to regularly post and post frequently.

If you have the right quality and that it is of sufficient quality to encourage interactions, you should not have any issues with this. But, if you simply post content with no interest, Facebook may effectively penalize you. If you feel that very few of your followers are paying attention to your content you should be patient until Facebook punishes you for low engagement. Then, fewer people are likely to be able to see your content after the penalization.

The next step is to get clicks on the sales pages. This is how you get subscribers to your list. Finally, you automatically publish your newsletters and get conversions on a regular basis. This is how you work. You basically send emails to your list of subscribers in an automated manner. This is the method you use to guide people to the post using ads or send them to sales pages.

If you're offering your own products and people buy anything, you get all the money they have spent. Plan your overall Facebook viral strategy based on the same pattern that I mentioned above.

Chapter 9: Share Viral Content On Twitter

How to share viral content on Twitter

Create the latest viral Twitter content to the Twitter timeline. After you've posted the latest viral video, hyperlink or image, add a tag to prominent profiles that are in your field. These are the people who are following this type of content. Tag them so that they can get their interest. If you've conducted your research correctly it is important to know the people who are.

It is likely that you are sharing a little of their content simultaneously. At now, you know what niche-related hashtags that people interested in the content you publish might utilize. Make use of these hashtags. The most important thing is to use HootSuite or another type of auto-publishing tool to organize your hashtag.

I cannot emphasize this enough. It is important to reorient your hashtags. Why? When people are interested in a specific area or a narrow number of subjects using hashtags. They are like the keywords you're focusing on. The problem is, you're not sure what hashtags will draw the most attention. It's a complete mystery.

This is why you should reorient your hashtags. In the event that you look over your stats and figure the frequency of traffic coming from Twitter and you are able to connect the dots. You should be able to make an educated guess at the particular hashtag set that was the source of the beautiful traffic and search.

Do not overlook the possibility of the possibility of revolving your hashtags. In the event that you fail to do so, it could be a missed opportunity. You'll make an error big time when you fail to use hashtags to your advantage. It is essential to know the most popular hashtags in your particular field. It's beneficial to continue collecting hashtag concepts and then revolving around them to determine which ones produce the greatest outcomes.

Create a Twitter Feed using Auto-publishing Resources like HootSuite

The best part about HootSuite is that it is capable of using an existing database file in CSV format. CSV format to input the content information. It isn't necessary to manually enter each piece of content you want HootSuite to publish for you.

If the application you're using is MS Excel and storing it in CSV CSV be sure that you're rotating your hashtags. Check to see if you're'resharing' or retweeting certain content and then turn your hashtags. Even if you're not retweeting content that has been curated You should still rotate your hashtags.

Another way to do this is to test things regularly out and observe the hashtag that is responsible for the wonderful increase in visitors your sales page has seen.

Do this while auto-publishing

While HootSuite is doing its work, you should not simply relax and wait for the money to come in. I'm sure that's the message many "make cash on the internet" ebooks and "online advertising riches" books instruct you to be expecting. This is the hype. It's certainly the ideal. However, they are often quite different from reality.

If you'd like your carefully curated viral content social media networks marketing strategy to be successful You must roll up your arms around and work in the background. Even if your content is auto-publishing, look up the profiles of your competition on Twitter. It is likely that you already have the following list. Take a look at their followers and make notes of those who are the most active ones.

They basically tweet every day, and then they are screened based on their particular niche. Take a look at the feeds on Twitter of these individuals. What are they most likely to tweet about? If you see an obvious connection between your work and what they're regularly tweeting or retweeting about, follow them.

It is crucial. Follow them. Here's how it can help you gain additional followers via Twitter. When people follow other accounts in a certain proportion, those they follow are likely to follow them in return. It's like saying "follow me , and you follow me." It all boils down to the principle of reciprocity.

It shouldn't be a surprise. It's a given that when you act in a positive manner toward someone, chances are pretty high that they will be likely to behave nice to you. This is how our brains are wired. When people follow you immediately on Twitter this is simply reciprocity taking place in the digital world. This is an extremely effective type of marketing because those who follow your back are more likely to be part of your segment of the market.

They are more likely to be curious about the information you're able to offer. In the future they could continue to see the tweets on your sales page for long enough times to become more involved. Keep in mind that the primary reason for the fact that the number of clickthroughs to Twitter is relatively low in comparison to other social media sites is due to the rule of 8.

Simply put, users are overwhelmed with the sheer volume of data through Twitter that they have to be exposed to the same piece of content over and over again in order to believe that it's okay to click it. In their minds, absolute familiarity means that in a way, the content is plausible to put a bet on it.

Whatever the situation may be, you must continue to retweet your posts using tools like HootSuite as well as following active followers of your competitors.

Keep your focus on the Strategy

It is vital to make sure that you auto-publish only specific niche-specific viral content. It is obvious this, however if you're not sure about the idea, you have ensure that all the content curated you're creating is right on target. They should be targeted to a specific niche.

Furthermore, they should be tested and verified or else, they've been retweeted or shared. This is second-hand material. It is not something that was just invented by someone. This content is being circulated since you realize that people have an some interest in it.

After that, you create an organic follower base of niche-specific followers through the process of reversing the followers of your competition simply by taking a look at your competitors by examining their followers' count, and picking their most niche-specific followers.

If your content is niche-specific and have a plan to add value to the lives of people looking at your information, don't be surprised by the fact that a substantial proportion of the people you follow will eventually follow your back. The trick here is to gain people who follow niches by using specific content that is niche-specific.

This can increase the likelihood of you being successful with your sales-page content. Naturally, there is no guarantee however in the event you take all the steps that were mentioned earlier and your fans are very niche-focused and devoted, the odds of turning them into customers can be very high.

\

Chapter 10: How Content Formats Can Help You Go Viral

Make sure your content formats are properly formatted to make it viral on multiple Platforms

If you can get the content on one website, and later posting it on another one, you will get a an adequate flow of traffic. Please note that what I've mentioned at least twice throughout this book that just because some content is popular on one platform, it does not mean it will be able to gain traction on another. Be aware of that.

To conclude there are a few common ways to share content across platforms.

YouTube Video Approach

The first thing you must accomplish is to find YouTube videos with an enormous amount of views. This is the first indicator of your success. This isn't some sleeper video. It's not one that was uploaded and then deleted. The video, actually receives a significant amount of attention within your YouTube segment.

After that, make note of the comments. How many comments do you have? In general, when people leave comments, it is a sign that they feel emotionally involved in the film. It could have reached them at a certain point or had an impact on them in a particular manner.

Whatever the reason the result was a positive one on the people. Look for high-comment videos and, finally, take a look at the number of likes.

It's not as important as the number of comments as well as the number of views. Also, you need to confirm that the YouTube videos that you are contemplating reposting are relevant to your particular niche. Once you've determined sure that this is the kind of video you'd like to collect, you can download the videos and post them with your Facebook and Twitter profiles.

Make sure that you are protected by mentioning CTTO as well as linking back to the YouTube channel from which it came. When sharing content on Twitter use the hashtag to turn around. Similar to this you can download Twitter and Facebook videos and then share it with YouTube. YouTube channel. This is basically carrying out actions reversed.

But, you'll need to protect yourself by posting an acknowledgement link alongside your CTTO text.

Image Strategy

Find viral infographics and images via Pinterest or Instagram. Use these to share with your friends on Twitter or Facebook with proper acknowledgement. The same applies to popular Facebook and images on Twitter however, you should do it on Instagram and Pinterest. Pinterest as well as Instagram networks. Also, make sure that you are circling your hashtags. Make sure that the content is special to the niche.

If you find viral content in your field in Facebook and Twitter Look for profiles in Instagram and Pinterest which pinpoint the specific niches. Follow their followers, and try to follow their followers and possibly invite the followers of yours to follow and follow you back. When you do this, you're taking your focus to two different levels. You're not just moving curated content around. Additionally, you're building an organic fan base for your profile.

All Content Must Be Ultimately Transferred into your Conversion Accounts

If you have a YouTube channel, it is essential have a link on your page, or your website. It might be located on your About page. It could also be included in the explanation for each video you upload to YouTube. Be aware that the vast majority of users do not visit the information page on YouTube. They might like the content, however may not take the time to learn more about you.

Do yourself a favor and make sure that every time you upload a video, you add your squeeze page's link or your website's URL in the description section.

Twitter Approach

When you are creating your profile on Twitter, make sure you have your squeeze page's URL or your website's URL on your bio page and make sure to include these links in the content you share. This is also applicable with your page on Facebook as well as the Facebook group posts. It's all about getting the most out of people who visit your squeeze page or homepage on your website.

As I've mentioned numerous times in this blog, when reposting content that you have curated it is essential to be involved. You shouldn't just take content that is well-known and simply move it to a different network, or redistribute it to the same network that the content is currently posted on. It's not likely to profit much from this content's viral appeal.

It is essential to test the headline, as well as the comments, and give the most value to each aspect of the material. As you can see, this will take some time, and this is why I would suggest that you employ an online assistant with solid English abilities from sites like Fiverr or, if you're trying to save money, cognoplus.com.

If you are in need of professional writing assistance You might want to take a look at Upwork or, if you're working on a tight budget however require top quality try ozki.org.

Chapter 11: Promotion And Sales

Instagram Promotion

We won't be able to purchase subscribers in this article. There's no need for dead souls. It's not at all difficult to figure out how the amount of subscribers is related to comments and likes. Twisted profiles are placed on blacklists, and the administrators of these accounts aren't considered to be trustworthy.

So, we'll eliminate shady schemes and provide methods that can earn your loyal customers and a high-quality target audience.

To spend less cost on advertising and marketing it is important to know the level of organic coverage an article is. Make sure that you do everything to ensure that the coverage increases. You always have the money to invest in advertising.

From March 15 to March 15th 2016 it was easy to navigate the Instagram feed. All posts were displayed according to the date they were posted.

The first posts are now appearing on your feed that the network considers interesting. What are the secrets of Instagram's Instagram algorithm, the creators have told reporters from techcrunch. The algorithm decides on what we find interesting and then shows it. Why is it important to be aware of Instagram's ranking criteria?

Take them into consideration when marketing their services and products. Thus, it is important to read attentively.

Every user's feed is constructed according to his behaviour in the app. That means that when you sign up to the same account as other users, you'll be provided with a unique feed of posts based on the way your interactions with the accounts. Explore more stories - they will be displayed to you. If you love the video, and Instagram will provide it to you. Don't forgetthat the algorithms of Instagram don't take into consideration the type of account used and the kind of content.

primary factors that define what users can are able to see on the screen:

1. Interest: To some degree, Instagram predicts how you think on the subject. A higher score will be attributable to those posts that are important to you. It is determined by your previous experience with similar posts.

2. The novelty: how long ago this post was written, and what is the prioritization for posts with new content over a period of weeks.

59

3. Relationships How close are you to the person who shared the post. A higher score is given to posts by people whom you frequently communicated previously via Instagram such as through comments on their posts or when you were linked in photos.

Three additional reasons:

* Frequency: How often do you log on to Instagram. It will attempt to display the most popular photos since the last time you visited.

"_. Followers: In the event that your account follows several individuals, Instagram will choose from more followers so that you see the smallest number of posts for each person.

* Use: how much the time that you use Instagram will determine whether you get the most interesting posts in short periods or whether the app expands your search in the event that you spend longer watching.

Instagram is a platform that considers engagement, which is the amount that reacts (likes or remarks) on your posts. This is why there is a massive "addiction" of Instagram users as well as the numerous jokes about the subject. Instagram displays the contents of the accounts that the user was active in communicating through conversations, commented and liked on posts. The speed at which people react to your posting can also play a part. If within a short time after the publication of your article, you receive social signals such as comments, likes and reposting and saving Instagram finds the post to be interesting and useful.

The Liketime event is for getting more likes. Account owners are in agreement to the date of posting and, after the post is published, all users on the list will like the posts of each other.

An Instagram spokesperson confirmed to Business Insider that the social media algorithm doesn't have one of popularity ratings. Posts that are less popular however, that are still important to the users will be shown in the high places.

Instagram account management strategy

The marketing strategy used on Instagram is comprised of a wide range of activities: starting with studying the audience you want to reach and your competitors as well as tuning your account, making a unique selling strategy by deciding on the visual elements and establishing your account. Of course, there are advertisements and engaging with opinion people.

In spite of its simplicity, Instagram is a serious tool. If you choose to connect with customers through the social media platform, you must prepare ahead.

Checklist for lazy people

1. Study the competition: Pay attention to the strategies they employ in their positioning. How do they reach out to customers, and what kind of activities are being carried out. Check out their blog articles and see which ones which get the most responses. It's recommended to create an Excel tablet Excel and then create these graphs.

* Name of the Competitor Account

* Product/service Prices, properties and discounts, loyalty system, loyalty rewards

* USP detuning: what is the main focus is

* Frequency of Posting

* What channels for promotion are they using such as targeted or blogging ads Does it participate in giveaways and is conducting mutual PR.

2. Consider what sets your product from your competitors What are your strengths and how can you impress customers and make your mark in the market. Create a list of your

advantages in advance. Based on these then, you'll create an advertising and content strategy. It is essential to study the objections of your competitors. Find them out and put them the account's details in separate posts.

3. Determine your target audience, what is important for them. Also, identify who they are, and what they consume.

4. Write down a list of topics that you'll write about, and the order in which the content will be rotated in order to not overwhelm people with posts selling and not disappear towards entertainment material.

5. Decide on your style - the way you present your content and the way you submit your text. It's also based on the audience you target and the type of content that will work in a competitive market.

6. Decide if you'll market your account. If so, it is important be aware of what that means and the amount of time you're willing devote to it.

Beginning working with Instagram is not the same as your initial post, and certainly not from the very first photography session, but rather with the right strategy. Before starting, you must analyze your Instagram account (if it already exists) like you did previously consider the advantages and disadvantages. This will aid in the creation of your strategy.

Goals. The first step is to determine the goals your account has: Are you working to enhance or establish a brand image for your company? Do you want to increase sales? Are you seeking recognition in Central Asia? Collect customer reviews to boost performance? Perhaps in one go, so why not.

Content After having looked over the image of the intended public (it must already be sketched out) Decide what content you're planning to release What, how, and how much.

Develop an outline of your content plan.Believe me working without one is extremely difficult. Writing content "on on the go" hasn't brought any much success until now. Content plans could be developed for one or two weeks, or one month. Based on your abilities (can you prepare topics and articles ahead of time).

Make a list of the "headings" you'll keep. This will allow you to manage your work. For instance, on a Friday you'll be discussing your team members using the hashtag #NAME_family and every Tuesday , you'll share the comments of the client on #NAME_about_us.

Indicators. Note down the indicators you'd like to reach within your account, such as the amount of subscribers and engagement, as well as reach the number of requests you want to target. The numbers you need to determine these are best measured through working for at least an entire period of a month, or even two. Don't just take numbers from your thoughts or your desire.

Promotion Methods. Think about what other Instagram promotion methods you will use: targeted advertising (budget, audience?) and opinion leaders (who and for how much?) and Contests (with who as well as how frequently) etc.

You must define your "roles" on the webpage. Who, besides you will have control of your accounts? Your assistant Your SMM manager? Someone who can take on comments? It is important to clearly define the responsibilities when there is multiple people in the team.

What are the best ways to advertise your business on Instagram?

We classify the promotions on Instagram into two major categories: low-budget techniques and advertising.

Low-budget methods

* Understanding and application of Instagram algorithm

* Cool content: in blog posts or stories, as well as highlights

* Use the recommended top of the list by hashtags, massfollowing

* Networking

* Activities: IFS and SFS on Instagram Flash mobs and marathons, contests, contests

* Mutopiar (cross-promo, guest blogging)

* Commenting

* Offline Promotion

Advertising

* Blogging

* The target is

Participation in the Giveaway (giva or Givavei)

A mix of strategies works best when you plan and continuously apply every technique while producing quality content. Photos that are well-thought out, thoughtful posts or stories that are funny will improve natural (natural) audience.

We've already spoken about how Instagram works and the Instagram algorithm, and the rules earlier. However, the conclusion about the algorithm's use are as the following:

1. Don't disappear from the feeds of your subscribers. Regularly updating your blog will make your brand more visible. Bloggers and marketers are encouraged to publish at least one article every day, and a few stories.

2. Engage your audience, improve interest, engage with your the subscribers.

3. Find out what interests the people who are watching. Track what triggers an increase in response. This could be photos video as well as short or long text information, or simply stunning images.

We will examine each method of marketing and you'll be able to determine where to begin the journey you're on with Instagram. We agree that there isn't a single recipe that works for all brands.

What can we do to make content useful for promotion?

Content plans are a publication plan for all Instagram channels you follow. These are posts that appear in your feed, stories and live broadcasts. It is also the content you are making for mutual PR or blogging promotions, and for video content on IGTV.

What's the reason? You have ideas to write about, don't ponder over the topic to write about even if you don't have the inspiration to write it all in the plan. Be careful not to skew entertainment content. Don't confuse yourself and don't forget.

Content types and categories depend on the type of account you're using. When creating a content plan:

* You won't forget about the Christmas season, and you can prepare special content ahead of time,

* You can get information on complicated topics in advance.

* You will easily work on an account with a designer/photographer/copywriter.

Determine the primary idea behind your material by answering What problem for your intended audience can you solve using your content? It is also worthwhile to look into the content of your competitors. You can search for them using the Instagram search engine for the most relevant queries.

What do you watch? What posts are liked and commented on more frequently, what type of comments they make, and what they have to say about (this could be a good topic for a blog post). You can look up hashtags that contain good content as an ideas and examples. Don't copy someone else Look for inspiration and improve. This can be done with Popsters which is a social media service for analyzing content.

Tip: create your content plan where it is convenient to you: in an individual notebook or the Trello service, table. Utilize spreadsheets within Google Docs. The access to content plans can be accessible from any device and you'll never lose any data. It's relaxing

The optimal frequency of posts:

Tape:

1. Business accounts: maximum 2 per day, minimum 1 per day.

2. Bloggers are 2 to 4 people per day.

Posts from the story:

1. Entertainment accounts: 1-10 per day.

Two. Business accounts 1 to 3 accounts per day.

3. Bloggers: 1-10 per day.

How do you make use of Stories as well as Highlights to boost your Instagram?

Storys is a great instrument for advertising and engagement Fixed stories can aid you in presenting your idea.

What can you publish in Stories

* You can thank members (increasing loyalties).

* Inform people about the promotion and only available today.

Display a new product.

* Display product history

* Short interviews, user stories

* You are able to discuss the contest and invite others to be a part of it.

Conduct a poll and then discuss the findings

* Watch an episode of a mini-series

Create a consistent stories section, such as questions or tips

What can you pin to Highlights?

* Brand Story/About Me/Acquaintance

* Delivery conditions

The terms of the payment

* Reviews

The shares and the terms

* Loyalty program

* Description of the Top Products

* Prices

* Heading of the account

* Thematic product choices

* Product Recommendations

* Review and Comparisons

Contact information for potential partners

* Conditions of advertising and PR mutually on your account

FAQs for frequently asked questions

* Examples of advertisements in publications

* Promotional Quests and Codes

* Master classes

* Free Utilities

It is now possible to set a timer for stocks. The hashtags in the story can be clicked.

Hashtags

What are hashtags and why do they necessary? It is word which is then followed by a pound sign (#). When you mark #, the phrase transforms into an hyperlink that can be clicked. When clicking on a link, the user is taken to into the message feed which have been labeled by this hashtag. Hashtags work with all social networks.

How can hashtags assist you to get ahead?

If you choose the right hashtags in your post You are more likely to experience higher engagement. This is because hashtags categorize the content and make it searchable.

Which are your most widely used hashtags?

* To take part in the search

* To record participation in marathons and in competitions.

* To access your account

* To advertise the brand

* For filtering of the product

* For quests , games and other games.

It is now believed that promoting through tags isn't efficient However, they must be added to your categories at the beginning of your campaign. Your content could be displayed in the stream of users even when they don't follow you. If you post great content and tag it using relevant hashtags, a lot users will begin following you.

Hashtags can draw interest to an organization, an event or event alone, trending, increasing audience reach and awareness of the brand.

You can create your own hashtag for your brand. Additionally, you can join hashtags.

A good example of the work by the creator's hashtag #evinsense

This is a two-way street When a users click on the hashtag, and then realizes that he is not happy with the hashtag's content, he may select an option "Do not display for the hashtag" in the settings.

There are three categories of hashtag frequency:

1. High Frequency - More than 1,000,000 Publications

2. Mid-frequency - frequency of more than 10,000

3. Low frequency - greater than 500

The high-frequency tag doesn't last long because each time someone posts a blog using this tag. It is better to use medium or low-frequency hashtags and mix them up with your own unique hashtags.

It's not an issue of being noticed by a lot of people, but getting noticed by only the right people. This is why hashtags boost engagement.

There are a number of important hashtag-related questions that novices frequently have to ask:

1. Can you measure the efficacy of hashtags?

If you've got a professional profile and you have a business profile, then yes.

2. How do you incorporate hashtags into your the story?

It is possible to add hashtags to your story using two methods - via the hashtag sticker or by using text. They work in the same manner as the stories.

3. What hashtags can be utilized in a typical blog post, and how many can be used in a stories?

The hashtag count can reach 30 in a normal post (studies show that the best number of hashtags is 9) and as high as 10 hashtags in story. We recommend that you minimize the number of hashtags used in your story or conceal their location behind the stickers. They will not bother people.

4. How do you find the most effective hashtags to promote your brand?

For a look at your other competitors, or media professionals from your field, go through Instagram's search results under the "Tags" tab. You can, for instance, use Tagblender's service. To select a suitable hashtag it is necessary to think about what phrase or word you're searching for the correct information. You can test the hashtag's compatibility to your content on Google.

5. What are the hashtags that are similar?

If you are searching for any hashtag on Instagram search, just above the top as well as Recent tabs, you will find a list of similar hashtags which you can scroll through by moving your finger to the left. This is a great way to find relevant hashtags that are special. This means that you've discovered a target group with less competition.

6. Where can I use hashtags?

Within the text of the article At the end of the post, in the first comment following the post. If you post them immediately after publication, hashtags are used in comments.

Hashtags 2019

On Instagram hashtags have always held significance. There is a belief that well chosen hashtags will not only bring customers and subscribers but also peace and harmony in your house.

However, this isn't the case. In contrast to the English-speaking world hashtags are not as powerful. ability and don't bring in subscribers in large quantities. In the same way hashtags that are related to women's beauty as well as geo-referencing, could be a great way to reach the desired audience and order. However, don't expect kitchen doors to be able to offer at the very least one glance.

The other point: pictures of posts where hundreds of thousands of views resulted from hashtags are widely used and "should be able to demonstrate the real potential of hashtags to those who are skeptical." This is wonderful, but no one needs coverage to be able to provide coverage. Coverage should result in sales or subscribers or engagement, provided that we're talking about huge FMCG brands.

This kind of viral coverage (the post got the most recommended post via the hashtag) of 200-300k followers could result in twelve users from any part of the world as well as ER Reach to a amount of 0.5 percent (with the typical 10-20 percent).

So, hashtags be effective in a small amount of niches. Hence, praying for them isn't worthwhile, but it's not mandatory to ignore them. It's a free tool which can provide some benefit, and it's foolish to ignore it.

Alongside numbers and letters hashtags also include Emojis. However, special characters and spaces like $ or %, will not work.

Mutual PR

The mutual public relations (VP) as well as friendly marketing are among the most cost-effective ways to advertise Instagram. Instagram. A few guidelines to follow for a successful VP

* The intended audiences of accounts who are advertising one another must be similar. Not necessarily, but extremely alike. For instance the local fitness instructor can advertise an account for local stylist and photographer. They are not competitors however, the target market is extremely alike.

* You must offer mutual PR to accounts which are similar to yours in terms of the number of subscribers as well as involvement.

* Mutual PR shouldn't be used for a purpose that isn't beneficial, as instead of growing customers, they'll be losing a few of them.

* It is recommended to ensure that VP articles aren't released on the same day.

* Make sure that your account is in order before searching for a potential partner for mutual PR.

* Go through the profile of the potential partner to see how do they respond, get involved, share and even like. Take a look at the bland and unremarkable comments that are in the "come on"come on it's awesome" style. Remember that likes as well as comments are bundled by special services. You can request figures.

Where can you find potential partners to collaborate on PR? Find out who your followers are following, and look for matches. Join Instagram chats on Telegrams and then search on there. Check out special services: Epicstars and inblogs.

If you plan to operate an airspace continuously, it is best to design specific sections. For example , # ask_special. Mutual PR can now be conducted in the form of a story or on the air when you invite a fascinating person to ask questions.

What can you do? In advance, announce the guest, but be sure to remember the announcement that will be made in just a few hours. When you are on air, and the guest will appear on your show and then click"Join" "Join" button. You agree with his request - cheers! you're now on air. If a blogger announces an event about you, and you announce it concerning him (only after a while and immediately and not worth the effort, this undermines trust). Try it.

Commenting and networking

It was not a possibility that Telegram could provide active support system for Instagrammers. A collection of bots that are useful that you found above. However, the most effective for those looking to get better at Instagram or assist others in doing it is instats-chats.

Encouragement of light times, discussions of blogging with bloggers (and the wholesale purchase of advertising from bloggers) Search for partners, fresh ideas, discussions about difficult times - all of that happens within chatrooms.

Insta-marketer, Bright-mind the founder of the School of Entrepreneurship on Instagram and the writer of the book "How to earn money from Instagram"

What exactly is network? It's the creation of important contacts, relationships and friendships. Nowadays all communication is almost entirely shifted to chat rooms.

You can find accounts with people share a common public, and whose accounts fall in similar "weight category" in terms of users. Chat owners with such accounts are able to learn about and plan any event that is beneficial to everyone involved such as a competition that is joint or marathon. You can see that you can exchange audiences and promote engagement.

Let's add up the benefits that result from networking active:

* You receive subscribers for no cost.

* People who follow your activities, discover that you are fun and cool, you provide some benefits. They then become regular subscribers. You're aware that involvement is the key to a sale (sooner and later).

* VP is this is the popular term used to describe mutually-owned PR. But! I would advise you not to make a promotion by introducing a new

partner on that day. Let him speak about your day today (in an article or story) and you will talk about him in the next week.

Communication is a great source of work. In other words it's not necessary to join chat rooms or a group of people who are looking for a way to purchase advertising at a lower cost or arrange joint activities.

Which chats are worth investigating first? These are useful passwords and addresses Try to share them with others about them.

* networkingDariaManelova

* chat_dnative

* In Showchat

* instasoft.ru

* from Berek

* inst_admins

* xmedia_chat

This is a great example of networking directly within your account. The posts that you post increase engagement and get a lot of views and views. They are effective, and your subscribers respond in a way that is active.

Commenting actively of blog posts (commenting) can be a means to increase your reach that is ideal for people who spend long hours on Instagram. Get familiar with the process of searching by hand and also increase the reach of their account.

The purpose of commenting is to leave genuine and relevant comments on the topic of the blog post from top bloggers and readers. There is no need to say "I sell cool clothing" it's spam. Be sure to write your answer clearly and in a meaningful way. For instance, you might sell bicycles. A well-known blogger says that he purchased a bicycle for a young child. In the comments, provide, without selling the bikes you are available, and what's the best option.

When posting comments, your personal participation in the conversation (without linking third party services) and a quick responses are crucial.

Offline account promotion

A non-traditional business, like such as a showroom, store cafe and photo studio, or beauty salon, offers the potential to draw customers who are not part of the network. A photophone with a logo or hashtag made of plastic or wood, and "selfie corners" assist in attracting new customers.

The Instagram Business Cards (nametag) is another method to draw people offline. Nametag is a type of QR codes. Business cards can be sent to family, friends clients, customers, or partners via messengers to create posters or stickers using the business card. It can also be used to print on souvenir items.

For a card to be scanned for a business you have to go to instagramand go to your profile, then menu> instagram business card> scan Instagram-business card. The phone should be pointed at your business card, and your profile will be displayed.

How to go about it:

Click on your "Instagram professional card" section, and choose the background for your business card. Then, you can download the company card to a photo or immediately share it via mail through instant messengers, or through social networks.

Mass-following and Mass Liking

Massfollowingis a huge number of accounts on Instagram that are subscribed to of other users. This practice has a basic purpose - to get reciprocal or reciprocal subscriptions. At the very least, you will get the number of views on your profile and clicks on the advertisement link within the description.

Mass-sharing is the same as mass-following but rather than subscriptions you can put likes in.

You can subscribe manually and also like it in a manual way however, they usually make use of special software that will automate the same action with scripts. Thus, you'll will save time and can select the right audience for your needs best.

These techniques were at their height of popularity just two years ago. The picture has since changed. Not all Instagram experts recommend them due to the potential for blocking.

The official website of Instagram is against the use these services and warns users that they could block your account. We don't call you to take these actions, but we would like you to be aware of the extent of responsibility when using these methods.

However, what experts are saying:

Mass follow-up and mass laking. The mechanisms are not the same as they were ago, however, despite the predictions, they're still going strong and are even bringing customers. My opinion is that it's a good choice for small-scale regional businesses as well as new bloggers. For cities with more than one million I don't recommend branding - it's difficult to connect with the right people, and even those who think they are can be shocked to learn that they've been loved by a local service or an established coffee shop chain.

Another issue with mass follow-up is that if it operates in tandem, or if there is traffic coming from bloggers it is difficult to monitor the effectivity. For instance, with the mass follow-up, you'll get a flurry of subscribers, but you require more than just numbers. Connect to the newsletter and inquire how the subscriber came to know concerning the subscription, however I've seen them forget about it and write "saw on Instagram"

Massfollowing and massliking phenomenon? What is the relationship between him?

ML and MF Today, ML and MF are not an "phenomenon" however, it's an established method of promotion, such as Instagram, VK, Twitter. If we concentrate on the mechanism, the process of mass-liking and subscribing is commonplace for anyone looking to build a network of contacts, and not just for marketer. One of the best examples is LinkedIn. I'm sure that many of us have been able to push promising HR professionals or employers, as well, people we were interested in. MF as well as ML are the most common methods for anyone who wishes to attract attention to themselves and their work, particularly as they produce tangible results.

We offer very affordable advertising contacts. They have the capability of "reach to", "reach out" to users who in a different circumstance would be inaccessible because it is physically impossible to connect with large audiences manually. With ML, you are able to draw a large amount of subscribers or customers to make money from your account. However, to achieve the desired result you must put in some hundred likes each day, which is difficult to manage manually.

In actuality, we're discussing optimizing the processes that you can carry out with your hands. Find users that might like your service or service, add them to your account directly, write them in direct or in direct. We help the many experts working with Instagram individuals, SMM experts, and digital marketing, and more for extremely reasonable money . This is our business. He is also honest.

Inflicts sanctions on Instagram for mass follow or mass link , or does it not?

The most severe penalty for Instagram is the perpetual ban. Based on our data as compared to conditions of 2016-2017, this measure of the impact on users is hardly utilized. The percentage of continuous bans in our customers is 0.03 percent. This is entirely within the error of statistical analysis therefore we aren't shy to speak about these figures. If you use MF or ML, temporary blocks are frequently encountered.

For this service allow users to assess and select the level of risk which they will take on. Instaplus.me service lets you decide on the degree of your promotion that is completely secure, safe and quick. This, naturally is not safe. However, we will inform users of this in the app.

Does it make sense to apply massfollowing or masslinking? If so, how? If so, how?

To be completely objective, it all depends on the reason for the promotion. If the client is looking to acquire many thousands of customers over an extremely short amount of time, for instance, six months, then you will need be aware of other options, for instance, massive advertising using popular accounts.

It is important to remember that MF and ML do not provide an answer to all problems. It is all dependent on the specific objectives of the company whether you sell products and to whom you sell it, through the Instagram account. MF and ML enable you to swiftly sign up active users, then turn them into customers, and utilize them to later monetize the Instagram page. MF and ML have obvious advantages, including speedy promotion of accounts as well as the capability to draw in their target users, high conversion. ML is a good option when the aim is to improve the loyalty of customers through "clicking through" their latest images.

It is not necessary to limit yourself to only MF and ML. For a complete promotion of your company through the Internet but this isn't enough. It is important to pay attention to other areassuch as PPC, SEO, PR.

Blogger Ads

The reach of blogging advertising is increased and provides a steady flow of readers. Blogging-related advertising is also known as"fluid marketing" as well as opinion-makers are known as influencers (from English influence - "influence").

Statistics confirm the power of influence from marketing:

77% of marketing professionals believe influence marketing to be appropriate for increasing the reach of their audience.

77% of consumers in the millennial age group trust the advice of acquaintances and family members. A similar survey found 70% of people prefer buying the product that is suggested by a non-professional blogger.

Who are bloggers for?

This type of advertising is great when it is in places where consumers can view the product. Big brands hire top bloggers to help promote new products, to maintain or build the brand's popularity.

Where can I find a suitable blogger?

You can delegate the search and interaction with bloggers to the agency. Search through special exchanges, pick by hand (look at the subscribers of your customers and research who is significant to them) and search chat rooms for ads as per guidelines.

Popular blogger exchanges:

* Epicstars

* Getblogger

* Sotiate.ru

* Plibber

* Labeling

* Inblogs

How do you determine if an individual blogger is suitable?

Request to display account statistics to assess the credibility of your audience.

Examine the level of engagement of readers of opinion leaders. Are there live discussions, do users of the blog pose questions? Are they different or similar for all posts.

Check out how often bloggers advertise the blog, and then how users react, especially in the event that they're outraged.

Think about the geographic location of the blog's subscribers when you are looking to promote a local business

Who are the most influential micro-influencers and bloggers?

Today, the top blogs are on Instagram and YouTube have over one million subscribers. Advertising with these opinion leaders can cost anywhere from 300 000 - 1 million 200 000 rubles.

Someone who has only a tiny, possibly 20 thousand followers and has a good level of involvement with no bots is active, active and a microinfluencer.

What is the price for the post and the terms of accommodation?

Contact the blogger's agent or. Usually, contact information is on the profile's header. Be aware that some bloggers may not respond promptly or even not at all. Some bloggers are able to create a line-up for placement while others focus on certain details or work, for instance in conjunction with big brands.

Most often, advertisements posted from a variety of bloggers with an audience of around 2-4 thousand subscribers provide more advantages than expensive advertisements from an elite blogger.

If a blog has an audience of a smaller size it is more hospitable as the writer of this type of blog communicates with the readers personally and responds to any comments. The degree of trust that is placed on the author of a blog is higher and the amount of engagement.

Story advertising is generally more affordable than advertisement.

Who is responsible for the promotional text that is used for publication?

It is important to describe your service or product it's properties, benefits and benefits, as well as your offer (offer). Bloggers generally will modify your content to fit your style. Offer physical items as a an incentive to advertise (barter) and to demonstrate on your blog.

I suggest you trust influenza marketing to a professional agency, especially if the business owner did not have an interest in the subject before. In this field observation and negotiation are crucial. Let me explain why.

Watchfulness. Look for opinions on the blogs from other blogs. When a manager frequently participates with the bloggers in the community it is clear who is talking to who, and which bloggers are a part of one another. In the telegram, there are numerous chats that are specific to One of most well-known is Instagram which is where bloggers leave feedback about advertising from bloggers. In reality, there's plenty of information available and new bloggers emerge every day and it's difficult to select the best 10 to launch a brand new project. In our company the manager searches for bloggers, asks for up-to-date information, checks for the status of their payrolls via Livedayun and manually reviews commentators, and examines the quality of their comments and seeks comments from past advertisers. Then , he talks about the conditions of cooperation and approves the blogger in consultation with the customer, supervises the payment process for the blogger or sending the products and agrees with the content and content, and controls the time of exiting the post , and assesses the outcome. After the campaign, a report is prepared. All these steps could take several weeks.

The ability to negotiate. There are a variety of delicate points in interacting with bloggers: discussions on barter, requests for a discount or another story, or a critique of the creative work. Each of these phases there is the possibility of some controversy or be a target for attention at the blogger's social gathering, and also be criticized by his followers. If you are a novice project this could result in disastrous. Some examples from the real world, but not from our organization:

* A blogger is presented with clothing with the words "gift" then within a few days, they need to write a blog or a story. A blogger (nearly half

million fans) is furious and screams at viewers to not follow the brand

* Friendship is provided to bloggers as a reward for a gift as well as a blog. If a blogger expressly states that only a story is able to be the basis for this offer the brand is accused of being a commercialist, unwillingness to make friends and starts to act rude. This is why the blogger community is unable to collaborate with the brand.

This is what we require - knowledgeable community managers will decide on the most appropriate terms for advertising and and then define the terms of reference to create the best imaginative, smooth any sharp edges and ensure that the client gets the best advertising results and positive reviews from bloggers in his social circle . If the brand is regularly involved in marketing that is based on influenza in the future, eventually, a group of loyal bloggers and perhaps, brand ambassadors will form who will start to promote to attract attention or at a more favorable rate.

Game mechanics and Instagram activity

Diverse rallies, events, marathons can energize the audience and draw new members.

Marathons This method in attracting followers is being employed on Instagram. Marathons are an interest group, and often, participation is paid. Bloggers gather, hand an abundance of helpful information, assign tasks, and then the participants post the results on their blogs. You can organize the race of the marathon or support the efforts of other participants. From you - donations and from the runners - advertising.

Practical jokes. Rewards for comments or reposts. Participation should be easy and tailored to the social media platform Instagram. You can request to repost the post as part of an article or make comments.

Flash mobs.They appear like marathons, but however, flash mobs are not charged for participants. The outcomes of your actions must be displayed on your personal profile, with specific hashtags, and the reach is increased. To draw attention to your profile you could be the host or host of the flash mob. You can also give a great prize. For instance, MiF publisher arranges excellent flash mobs and assigns individuals tasks who participate, and prize winners are given books. Here's an example the challenges that the publishing house has set. The results by using the hashtag #mif_challenge.

We sought an expert's opinion on his experience of conducting competitions.

Competition Mechanics

It is a great method to simultaneously boost engagement, increase the reach of your profile and also attract new subscribers. Pros:

It is more straightforward than, for instance creating an advertising campaign, particularly if you are a novice and don't know the settings for targeting.

* The contest can be conducted with a minimal cost of investment: to spend to promote announcements on the internet and an additional cost, a prize item or your time, if you're participating in an activity.

Minuses:

* During the contest, freeloaders may appear, who sign up for only the chance to win, and remove themselves from the list after the draw.

* The second point from the initial one is an unsubscription wave that can impede the coverage on the profile.

How to limit the influx of freeloaders: advertise an article that is competitive to your most targeted public (interests or age) and, in the case of an local business, be sure to include a geo). If you've got limited accounts the number of freeloaders , and the subsequent unsubscribes will likely to be low. In any event, in the course of the competition, new customers have to be included.

How to accomplish it:

Participate in the discussion. It is the easiest way for you to have questions asked at the close of your post. However, for this it is important to understand the needs of your readers to ensure that your questions don't appear fake (people believe they are fake) And, the readers were keen to voice their opinions.

* Write a post-acquaintance to ensure that newcomers can easily navigate through your account. If you're using an automated rubricator (if not, buy it) add the hashtags for navigation so that your subscribers are able to find interesting content.

• Remove stories. Unlike stories in the feed, it's more difficult to miss. "Stories" provide real-world examples (admit who doesn't like to look into the lives of your favorite bloggers?) and also interact as the result of a series. So, they must be removed on a regular basis.

How to run an event that is successful A checklist

1. Choose a prize or prizes that will benefit your target audience. For example, if , for instance, you own a beauty salon and you are not playing with hair dye. Your customers are likely not going to need the product (real instance). In exchange for a prize you could get the benefit of a discounted item or service, or even a complimentary product or service, based on the desires and requirements that are common to Central Asia.

2. Set clear rules for participation. Realistic mechanics - post the announcement of the contest in the history of the contest. It's not hard, and unnecessary publication won't block your profile as a contestant and provides the opportunity for coverage and virality. The only downside is that the article disappears within 24 hours, which means you'll either have to make an effort to highlight it throughout the contest, or put those who participated on the table as soon as possible after the notice about repost goes directly to the person who posted it.

The most popular options are to comment on an article that is competitive or to mark three or more friends. In the first you'll see more participation and, in the second case, the involvement and the possibility of virality. You can mix mechanics, as For instance, One Two Trip did. However, the more difficult the requirements are for participation, the higher the prize.

Another intriguing technique that OneTwoTrip also employed was the setting of the topic for comments. Participants do not just post a comment to the sake of it and they also share their thoughts (and lots of people love to voice their opinions, and it's great when a company or blogger asks about it) or, in the case of an article from an example create an idea for a story. This way you can have an entire chat that includes heart-to-heart conversations. For example, in just 14 hours, more than 3,000 posts will be submitted in a contest's post.

You could use a nifty strategy; include the condition that the more participants leave comments, the greater chances of winning. Use the STOP mechanism - when, you set a time but not being known by the contestants you put "stop" within the post. The person whose comment is the last to be left before him wins.

3. Make sure you include an article on promotion without it, 3 to 10 percent of subscribers will get to see the contest. If you have the funds during the time of the contest you may be able to purchase advertising through a blogger. If not, you must set the rules for participation to ensure maximum viability: share stories or friend's marks.

4. The winners should be announced in a way that people are convinced their fairness in the drawing. It is possible to present a live broadcast or record the process in video and include it into the article. Note the account of the winners, and make sure to mention in the contest's announcement that the drawing has ended It happened where new subscribers discovered an old publication and began taking part.

Bonus - How to identify the winner:

The simplest method to use is to choose the random-number generator.

1. Upload all comments made under the contest's post to the ex-table using through the LiveDune service. You can try the free trial or purchase access to a single account with 300 rubles. Every participant will be assigned an identifier in the table.

2. Start a sequence of numbers between 1 and randomly generated number generator (here replace for the participants' number from the table) and then click "generate". The final number can be displayed or recorded in a video of the entire process.

3. Find the desired numbers in the chart, then highlight it in colour, and then go to the account of the contestant on Instagram and confirm whether he's met all the conditions of competition. Yes? You're won! Not? Make a new one. The procedure of determining the winner of the table is also recorded on video.

4. You can mount two videos at once or make use of the Unfold application. There are templates that let you put two videos on the screen.

5. Write a story and then mark the winner. The contest will be held!

Extra tip: don't play the draw too often, as you risk the risk of having the freeloaders and devaluing the item or service as people will not buy it, and you'll have to wait for the next draw

Promotion of posts and targeted ads on Instagram

The main point is that you create the audience you wish to reach with your advertisement to and the goal of this is to attract applications and generate sales. Blogger advertising and competitive mechanics are more effective for the growth of users on Instagram.

If you have a business profile, you are able to "raise" the possibility of a separate blog message to a specific audience directly through the application In the same spot, select an advertising budget, and include a payment option.

Insta marketers do not advocate this approach. It's simpler to use, however with the aid in the area of Facebook accounts, it is possible that you can get greater results at a lower cost.

Advertising that is targeted

The principal goal in targeted ads is convey your message to a particular group of people (time zone, geographic location or location, age, social status and gender, as well as the interests of the audience you decide). In other words, you market the product or service to prospective buyers.

Your ideal target audience is young women living in a specific city? If you have the right settings, they'll only be able to view ads.

Instagram is targeting certain types of users

Geographic targeting displays ads that are relevant to the region, from whole countries , to a specific store or cafe.

Demographic targeting chooses people based on gender and marital status, as well as age as well as the presence of children as their age. You can display ads to people who recently relocated or are soon celebrating the birthday of their choice and also to travelers.

Social targeting groups users according to the level of education (from students to doctoral student) or the direction in which they study, or educational institution. Under"work," in the "work" part, you can target the employer, a particular sector and job.

Interest targeting allows you to choose those who are interested in a particular hobby or have a hobby. This option is a form of test for the understanding of your client.

The fundamental principles behind targeted advertising

For accounts with Facebook as well as Instagram you can have one account. It may be surprising to some however Instagram is controlled by Facebook since 2012.

*The proper time zone. Make sure to pay attention when you are setting your advertising account in case the advertisement is not set correctly, it will be removed when your customers are asleep.

*Currency of payment : make sure to ensure that the currency you require is specified.

*Money from Facebook is not wiped out prior to the advertisement campaign, however, it is a matter of time after the results.

Be sure to establish the amount of money you will spend. Particularly important for novices.

If you operate offline businesses you can create a custom advertisement for the people who live in your town or even your area.

Placement is the location in which advertisements will be displayed. Instagram - Placement.

*You can be paid per click (CPC) or impressions (CPM).

Advertisements must be evaluated, some of them must be removed to ensure the best results while the rest must be disabled. Yes, the tests must also be given an amount.

In the advertising office, the roles are as follows: analyst (observer), advertiser - owner of page that include analyst (observer) advertising (owner of the page) (the most authority, who can make adjustments to the program) and an administrator (wide authority to initiate advertisements and to add administrators).

*Facebook keeps track of the users who contacted you and creates an audience that resembles yours. This is an excellent promotional tool.

How can I tell if I require targeted advertising?

Insta-marketer, Bright-mind creator of the School of Entrepreneurship on Instagram and the author of the book "How to make money with Instagram"

The targeted advertising method doesn't work efficiently on Instagram in just one situation that is a group of subscribers. Even then there are some exceptions for attracting subscribers to the blogger via advertisements in stories or by bringing readers to the blog through regular advertisements on the feed, for example. The target is perfect to sell on the website as well as for enlisting people for an event or newsletter that include inviting them to attend the initial free consultation, or for an offer to earn a reward with the first purchase.

There are times where targeted advertising is the only way to market it. Geo-referencing to dentists private clinics, private clinics food delivery, beauty salons, restaurants hotels, cafes etc. doesn't always permit working with bloggers whose audiences are larger than one city.

Before you start planning an advertisement, you should be familiar with the rules of Facebook for the dimensions and quality of the advertising materials as laid out in their official guidelines. There are cases that discuss the usage of different advertisements.

Analytics on Instagram for Instagram

A unique scenario is that the analytics of both services and Instagram (in personal and business accounts) do not align. Marketers have said that analytics on Instagram themselves aren't perfect but the other attributes of applications and services are worth every penny. The analysis of the various services can be found below. While we wait we will discuss the specifics of what should be examined.

The opinion of the experts is that you should be paying attention firstly to the clicks you make on the website (if there are sales through it) and to connect with (especially beneficial if your goal is to gain recognition) in addition to identify actions (requests through direct or comments). It is the way you determine the number of Instagram users that could eventually be your potential customers.

It is ideal to link website visits to the sales made on the site. Keep track of the user's activity and attempt to identify the connection between your website's content and user actions. For instance, if you have a promotion running examine the statistics on clicks. Also, look at the statistics for the number of orders.

These metrics will give you details about what content is most effectively in terms of sales.

Analytics Services for Instagram

This is a list of easy, quick and effective stats and analytics tools:

*Socialstats

Analyzing posts such as reposts, likes, photographs, subscribers' activity. A variety of filters for results, and statistics output.

*media-vk.com

Study of competitors, it is a portrait of the buyer. The cost for the service is paid by the client, and the price depend on the number people in the group you wish to study. You'll be able to identify the admins of which groups to work with so that you can place ads within groups.

*livedune.com

Provides the most precise information. Finds good advertising websites. The most adored Instagrammers. Chip - Search for opinions and leaders.

*Popsters

Social media analytics for content. Analyzes and compares the efficacy of the publications. Searches for entries using keywords simultaneously across all social media networks.

*Picalytics

Service deep analytics instagram accounts. It analyzes and collects data in three categories the audience (gender bots, real people, geographical, or other interest) engagement (total number of comments and likes on the account, and the average amount per post) Optimization (best time to post).

Summary

Like every other promotional tool, Instagram requires complex coordinated actions, well-thought-out strategies. It's a lot of work. You won't even realize how much time you've wasted. And the results of this labor won't be a problem. Incorporate Instagram as part of your marketing plan Make it a complete sales channel, make money from your blogs, increase the number of followers and let it work to benefit you.

Chapter 12: Marketing By Mail

Mail marketing is a means to reach out to customers quickly through electronic mail. While it's among the most seasoned players in virtual marketing, it's also one of the marketing channels with the most conversion rates. Campaigns via email are cheaper when opposed to other forms of advertising in terms of interaction with your clients and selling, as well as increasing your brand loyalty. It could also prove as a highly effective marketing tool for your commercial enterprise when paired with appropriate strategies.

A greater than one-third of the population in this sector has an email account.

Based on 2016 figures An average of the equivalent of 240 billion emails are delivered every day. The number of emails sent increased to 1.4 billion in 2009.

*The average office worker gets around 121 emails per every day. The average is 49.7 percent of those messages are spam.

*The beginning rate of receiving messages on mobile phones increased to 22 percent in the year 2012, and increased to 68% in 2016.

Automation-based emails increase sales by 320% than manually-generated email messages. (for example, sending computerized emails to remind users that they have purchased something from their shopping carts on an online store but haven't yet completed their purchase)

Let's examine the effects of evaluation on Pitchbox along with Backlinko over 12 million messages for 2019. The outcomes are as following:

1. Only 5 percent of emails were responded to.

2. E-mails that have an extended name are about 25% more likely to receive a reply than those with a short name.

3. Sending several email messages at the exact same time to the person increases the likelihood of obtaining solutions.

4. Personalized subjects boost responses by 30% and individualized mailer content increases response rates by 32%..

Social media

The idea of defining social media solely dependent on a limited number of channels might not be appropriate. These channels typically offer an opportunity for communication between users and manufacturers as well as to share your

111

thoughts, feelings or concepts immediately. It is possible to create profiles for your business or personal company on many social mediaplatforms, as well as share pictures, percentages, statuses ideas, etc. on. Immediately.

What is the difference between social media advertising and marketing?

Advertising on social media is among the advertising channels that use digital technology to market and sell products and services using social media platforms like Facebook, Instagram, Linkedin, Twitter. It could also include management of content on social media as well as direct advertising in the context of marketing and advertising on social media.

Social Media More Than Facebook!

In the above paragraph Social media is much more than the structures of Facebook, Instagram and Twitter. It is possible to say that almost every field has a social media outlet for their location of leisure. For instance, TripAdvisor as well as Airbnb are considered as social media platforms.

The growth in popularity of social media required marketers to offer innovative strategies. Social media marketing is a successful digital marketing and advertising tool that you can utilize to reach your final objectives, such as getting more customers to your website, increasing users to your site and presenting information about the latest products you offer, increasing revenue, and assisting your clients.

Around 87 percent of entrepreneurs believe social media advertising can increase sales.

Website

Websites remain the main form of digital marketing channels. A lot of advertising channels are utilized to draw users to go to the site. This seems to be the situation for the long time. I'd like to bring up one of the most significant issues that is evident within medium-sized businesses. I've observed companies that have a marketing budget for each month of 20-30 times the cost of the web website. In complete contrast to the user experience, mobile designs lead customers to their poor websites via advertisements. If they could design their website to be a people-oriented experience or create person-centered designs, they may be able to significantly increase conversion rates.

Facebook Advertising

Do you have to recharge the batteries to your ads you place on Facebook? With this Facebook Ads guide, you will be able to comprehend all you require to know to learn how to use this advertising tool beginning from scratch. You can then keep it in your ads even if you just invest one euro per day.

We'll start with the basics. After reviewing all the options that you will need to set up your campaigns, including illustrations and screenshots and will conclude with a thorough guideline for creating an effective Facebook advertisement step-by-step. Let's get started!

1. What are Facebook Ads?

Facebook Ads is the Facebook advertising platform. It is indeed the egg that is golden for this social media platform but the great thing about it is that it could be an excellent source of your marketing strategies online because it comes with many benefits, which we'll soon discover.

1.1 Why do you need to pay for ads if Facebook can be "free"?

You might be asking yourself one of the following questions Why do I need to spend money to advertise on Facebook If I already post what I want to for no cost?

Yes, creating your own fan profile through Facebook and sharing the publications you'd like to see is absolutely cost-free.

1. Can I make ads even if I don't have a page on Facebook?

For a powerful tool, Yes, you can put up an ad for Facebook even when you don't have an account. However, I don't recommend this because it has several limitations:

* You are able to display your advertisements on the right side. However, this means that they cannot be displayed via mobile phones (in another part within the Facebook Ads guide we will be discussing the various locations your ads might include).

* You can add an image within your advertisement (then we will see all available formats)

* You could aim at bringing customers to your site (then we will look at all the goals you could choose from).

However, if you're still looking to make an advertisement for Facebook without having any page, you are able to create one by logging into your Facebook profile and accessing the tool for creating ads. Below you'll find additional information on how to create an ad step-by-step .

2. The major benefits of Facebook ads are the main benefits.

I am a fervent Facebook Ads fan, primarily due to these reasons:

* Potential for Reach: Facebook has more than 1 billion active users. If you're looking to connect with potential customers using Facebook the tool will make it simple to locate them.

* Segmentation options: Facebook has immense information regarding its users, and it lets you refine the criteria for deciding who you'd like your ads to display.

* Controlling your investment: Facebook advertising is for any budget and you can manage your investments at all times. You can also keep track of the results to determine the effectiveness of your ads and alter your campaigns.

* Flexibility: You can make as many campaigns as you wish and choose from a variety of styles, and experiment with segmentation or end a campaign anytime you'd like.

3. Tools such as The Power Editor and Ad Manager

To manage and control our advertising campaigns, Facebook offers different tools:

Ad Manager

This tool is the central point of your marketing operations on Facebook. Through the Ads Manager, you can design ads to manage them, track the performance of your ads, etc.

It's a easy and intuitive tool that will guide your through each step in the procedure.

3.2 Power Editor

This tool is targeted at professional accounts with large amounts or who have multiple accounts. For example, an advertising and marketing agency who manages campaigns for many clients and requires to have greater control over ads and the outcomes of campaigns.

3.3 Business Manager

This tool lets companies share and manage the use of advertising account as well as Facebook pages more securely through one platform. Anyone who uses Business Manager is able to view all the advertising and pages accounts that he is working on from one central location.

4. The types of objectives and the kind of Facebook advertisements

When you are creating a campaign, it is important to first establish the goal of your campaign is. The goal might differ for each of the campaigns you run.

In the beginning, and based on the plan it is important to consider the following questions What do I hope to accomplish by releasing this announcement? What outcomes do I hope to see?

The basic goals anyone can pursue to use to advertise on Facebook are categorized into three categories:

* Recognition

* Prestige

* Conversion

4.1 Recognition

What you're looking for is to establish yourself to generate interest, and ensure that your brand's image begins to gain traction into the minds of your customers. The goal here isn't to directly sell something, but to market your brand by highlighting what you do and the way you conduct it.

In order to do this, you need to be focused on explaining the value your brand provides to people who are interested in you and what issues or requirements they have to help them and also highlight what is unique about your brand and sets you apart from your competition.

4.1.1 Brand Recognization

What's important to you is reaching those individuals who are likely to be linked to your brand and tend to be interested in your advertisements.

4.1.2 Local Broadcast

What you want is to get in touch with those who are near to your company with your advertising.

4.1.3 Scope

What you're hoping for is your advertisement to be seen to the most amount of people in order to get maximum exposure.

4.2 Prestige - Consideration

What you want is to boost the recognition of your brand's name among people who are already attracted by what you have to offer. Improve your reputation and create an increase in confidence.

In this case, you don't sell any product directly, but you are trying to get who will do something such as visiting your site, be followers of your Facebook page and so on. This is a second step, and they will then be potential customers.

4.2.1 Traffic

The goal is to draw visitors to your site or to a particular landing page , or for instance, to the Facebook store.

4.2.2 Interaction

What you're looking for is to attract more users to visit your website or publication and engage with them.

This goal for interaction could be more specific, based on your preferences at any moment:

* Interactions with a post : comments, likes and shares

* I love the Facebook page : gain more likes

• Event response : announce your event to increase attendance

* Requests for Offers to have more people request for discounts or offers

4.2.3 Generation of prospective customers

Make a list (information) of those who might be interested in your work or products you sell. In other words, those people you may offer your services to at some point.

4.2.4 Video views

Promote your videos to ensure that they are seen by more people , and improve the popularity and visibility for your company. We can discuss unique videos about your brand, content that is branded such as product launches or stories from customers.

4.2.5 Application Downloads

The aim is to get people on the site which allows you to download the mobile app.

4.3 Conversion

The purpose is transactional, because what you're searching for is to convince people who are interested in your business to purchase or employ your products or services. They can go to your store or use an offer code for discounts, etc.

4.3.1 Conversions

You are searching for users to take valuable actions on your site or application that you can measure.

4.3.2 Catalogue of sales

The goal is to advertise the catalog of your products. To achieve this, you need to make ads that will automatically display items from your catalog in accordance to the audience you want to reach with your campaign. This page provides instructions on how to build catalogs of your products .

4.3.3 Visits to the company

Your aim is to attract more customers to your establishment by reaching out to people located at a specific distance from one or more places of your business or restaurant, store and so on.

5. Facebook ads formats

Through Facebook ads, it is possible to create ads in a variety of formats that contain images, text videos, text, etc.

5.1 Photo Ads

As you've probably guessed, images are extremely effective. In this way, you can design ads that blend compelling text and a stunning images that draw interest.

5.2 Video Ads

A loud format. Video allows you to create a narrative by combining images as well as sound and movement. It allows you to showcase various aspects of the product. It also lets you offer a more personal experience to create more intimacy and emotion. It also increases confidence.

The videos look well. Based on Facebook's statistics over 100 million videos content are shown on Facebook each day.

5.3 Ads in Sequence

By using this format, it is possible to display multiple videos or images in the same advertisement.

5.4 Announcements and Presentations

By using this format, you can make a more simple video ad created from still images, or from an already existing.

This format was created to maximize the potential of video by spending less time and money in the process of creating it.

5.5 Canvas Ads

This particular advertising format, only available to display in mobile phones, has been intended to be an "personalized marketing experience." What exactly is that? It allows you to make full-screen video and image ads that include hyperlinks, text and call-to-action buttons that load 10 times quicker, Facebook says.

When you touch the screen, the advertisement can be tilted, enlarged or rotated. This means that you can interact with the ad. This is why you get"personalized experience" "personalized interaction".

5.6 Collections

This format that can display on smartphones lets you mix an image or video ad that can include up to four images of the product.

It's a method to make sure that the customers who you're talking to can easily find your services.

Design tips for Facebook ads

The tool itself provides us with suggestions on the quality and size of images and the size of the title and text as well as other suggestions. to ensure that our advertisements can be properly displayed on any page of Facebook.

It is essential to keep these tips in mind because you're the first to think about seeing your ads appear effectively. It will also affect the reach of the advertisement and in certain instances Facebook might even take you off the path.

These are the fundamental guidelines that Facebook offers:

* The recommended image size is 1200 628 pixels.

* Image Ratio: 1.9 1.

* Text: 90 characters.

* Title: 25 characters.

* Link description (if equipped): 30 characters.

* The image should contain only a few lines of text (0 there is no text)

6. Advertisement

With Facebook Ads, you are able to place your ad in various places:

* News Section: on the wall, mobile and desktop

* Right column will only be shown on computers.

* Instagram is mobile-only

* Audience Network: additional websites and mobile apps.

6.1 Automatic places

This is the option that is default. Facebook is also the company that decides the location where our ads will be displayed in all times to ensure they have better performance.

6.2 Edit places

Letting it fall into the hands of Facebook is typically a wise choice, as you need to be aware the fact that Facebook itself is keen on seeing your ads performing as efficiently as it is possible to keep investing in your campaigns.

However, if you wish to be in complete control you are able to specify where your ads to show. This can be done by clicking"Edit Locations. "Edit Locations" option.

When you click this option you will be able to select from:

* Type of device You can choose to have it to be shown to all devices, but just on computers or on mobile phones.

* Platformsinclude: Facebook, Instagram, Audience Network.

Optional options You can choose all mobile devices or select just Android or iOS as well as restrict categories so that your advertisements do not appear on apps or websites of a specific type of content.

7. How does ad targeting work on Facebook

Without doubt, the greatest strength of Facebook ads is the fact that we can make use of all the information we have about our audience, and test new audiences in order to design ads segmented to get the people we're most interested in.

Before you begin, you must get familiar with these ideas:

* Basic audiences segmentation of your target audience based on characteristics, demographics and behaviors, for example.

* Custom audience: Add details from contacts who you've already established contact

"Similar audiences: Add like-minded people in your list of contacts or customers

To create an PERSONALIZED PUBLIC it is possible to create a PERSONALIZED PUBLIC by using an image of your own clients to determine whether they're using Facebook or create an inventory of those who are the most active users of your content on Facebook or via your mobile app. For this you can choose to include telephone numbers, email addresses and Facebook usernames.

From there, you are able to create your own segmentation SIMILAR PUBLIC.

You may also build the audience you want to target for your campaign, or choose one you saved from a previous campaign.

This Facebook advertising tool lets users to segment their viewers based on the following guidelines:

7.1 Places

By using the geographical segmentation on Facebook you can choose provinces, countries, autonomies cities, postal codes, and cities as well as add more places. apply exclusion criteria if you do not want your advertisement to show up in a particular area.

Within this section you are able to select from a range of factors:

* All persons who are related to the specified location

* Residents of the same area

* Recent visitors who have been there

* Travelers who are passing through that area

7.2 Age

You can pick the age of people you wish to target with your advertisement.

The minimum age for a child is 13 years and the maximum age is 65 .

7.3 Sex

You can decide to display your ad to all, just females or men.

7.4 Languages

Most often, you'll want to choose to leave this field blank because Facebook will automatically use as a reference the language used in the area you've selected However, it also offers you the option of marking the language spoken by the group you wish to reach out to in the event that it doesn't match.

7.5 Detailed segmentation

With the help of segmentation in detail We can refine our communication the audience we want to reach by incorporating certain features:

* Demographic information: you can divide your data based on factors like academic qualifications and employment sentimental status, household composition , or the lifestyles of the people you're trying to reach.

• Interests. You are able to filter your audience according to their hobbies, interests and the pages they are most interested in on Facebook.

* Behavior: you are able to categorize your audience according to their preferences for shopping, their specific usage of their devices, or on the activities they engage in for example, whether they travel, go to events, etc.

Additional categories The Facebook's own categories.

7.6 Connections

This way you can categorize your visitors according to criteria related with the "connection" with your site:

* People who already follow your Facebook page.

* Friends of friends who have liked your page.

* Remove people who have liked your page.

The people who responded to your call

* Do not exclude those who have already replied to your announcement

If you choose one of the targets, Facebook will show you within a pop-up window with a column on the right the reach potential of your advertisement dependent upon the dimensions of your target audience.

Once you have completed the segmentation after which you must select "Save the audience". The audience you selected will be the recipients of your campaign. Its configuration will be saved in the event that you wish to use the segmentation again in the future campaigns you decide to run.

8. Calendar and budget

In the process of launching your advert when you are launching your ad, you should choose the budget as well as the calendar.

8.1 Set the limit for daily expenditure , or for the total campaign

Budget is the total amount you're willing spend each day or for the whole campaign depending on the time of your circulation. This way you determine and control what you'll spend on every campaign.

8.2 Select the ad's ad's time of the ad

The calendar defines the time that the announcement is circulated. You can decide to make it available for a period of time or choose a start and end date. You can alter this calendar any time you wish to extend the duration or end the campaign.

8.3 Optimization for ad delivery

Facebook allows us to select from three different types of optimizations to calculate the cost of our advertising performance based on our goal. For instance, if you're looking to increase traffic, you'll have the following choices:

* Users who click upon the links: Your advertisement will be shown to people the most likely click the link within your advertisement in either the Facebook app the site or offline Facebook.

* Impressions: the advertisement will be displayed as many times as it is feasible.

A single daily target: The ad will be displayed to the public at least once per day.

8.4 Bid amount Auctions in Facebook Ads

After deciding if we are looking for impressions or clicks The next step will be to determine the value of the bid. This will determine the efficacy of the bid. Facebook will optimize the distribution of our advertisement.

The bidding process is an online auction where our advertisements have to compete with other ads in order for the chance to be displayed to our targeted audience. other ads that match requirements to ours.

This is the reason, in order to ensure the highest performance of our advertisements against our competition, we need to create a competitive bid. or leave it to Facebook.

Here are two choices:

* Bidding that is automatic: Facebook is the one who determines the amount to allow you to receive the most impressions or clicks (views) for the lowest cost.

The manual bidding process is where You choose the highest amount you're willing to spend for each click (CPC) or per 1000 impressions (CPM). But, Facebook proposes an indicative amount, as well as the minimum and maximum.

The amount we ultimately choose will determine the amount we're willing to pay per click, or per 1000 impressions. However, the cost can be reduced when we do not face a lot of competition for the bid.

9. Measure and analyze the effectiveness of your advertisements

The process doesn't stop after making and launching an advertisement. Now is the time to test and assess how your campaign is performing for you!

Monitoring your ads and analysing the results will allow you to evaluate the effectiveness of your ads, evaluate the best and worst for you based on the various kinds of advertisements you create and re-orient your actions to improve the effectiveness of your investment

9.1 Analyze the impact of your marketing campaigns

In the Ad Manager itself you can keep track of the outcomes of your advertisements at any point according to the goals you've identified such as reach, clicks and interactions, visualisations of a video, the average cost per outcome (clicks and interactions, etc. ...).

9.2 Conversion Tracking Pixel

In order to track and assess your goals for conversion using an pixel for tracking conversions.

If you choose the "Conversions" goal and click the "Create an image" option will show up on the Ad Manager.

This pixel is a fragment that you need to insert on your website so that you can track your actions, monitor the effectiveness of your ads and improve your advertisements to improve conversions, and the remarketing (that the ad will be displayed to users who were interested but haven't yet completed what you're trying to find).

The pixel's name must be specified. One pixel can only be created for each advertising account.

10. How to create an advertisement on Facebook step-by-step

We are now ready to begin our work. We'll look at how to make an effective Facebook advertisement step-by-step and, to illustrate we will take an actual example. This is an advertisement to advertise my SEO free course XD.

Step 1. We connect to the Ad Manager via our Facebook account.

From our Facebook page In the upper right bar, we will be able to navigate to our options "Create ads" along with "Manage my Ads".

From there, you can directly gain access to the main panel that is the Ad Manager.

Step 2. We choose a goal for the campaign.

In this instance the goal will be contact with the magazine. In the same panel, we will give a name to the campaign.

Step 3. We determine the audience we want to target.

We use the following criteria for segmentation:

Place: All Spanish speaking countries

Gender: all

Age: We size to include people who have an age range of 18 and 50

Interests: In this instance, my interest is in all people who have expressed an curiosity about SEO.

Step 4. We decide on the location we'd like to advertise in.

I'm interested by the ads that is currently running on Facebook as well as on desktop smartphones and computers.

Step 5. We establish the budget and the period of circulation.

In this scenario we establish the maximum budget for each day and decide that the advertisement run for an indefinite period.

To optimize the display of advertisements we select the option "Interaction through the advertisement" in order that Facebook is accountable for displaying advertisements to people who are most likely to engage with the advertisement by clicking "me Like" or a shared comments.

Amount of bid is set to "automatic" mode to ensure the Facebook determines the price which allows us to get a larger quantity of interactions for the lowest cost.

In this scenario we will pay the amount of the bid automatically per thousand impressions (times our advertisement is displayed) but never exceeding the daily maximum budget we previously set.

Step 6. Start with the creation of an advertising page. Here we can choose to select to utilize an existing publication already published on our page on Facebook.

We can also create an entirely new advertisement this is the next thing we'll create the next time.

Step 7. Choose the format for your advertisement.

We choose the format of our ad. In this instance I'm looking for an ad that has only one image.

We pick the image we want to use and add the text (persuasive text that assists us to accomplish our objective).

We look at our previews of advertisement for both mobile and desktop versions to determine if we need to alter the ad.

Ready! We're ready to launch the advertisement!

The advertisements on these two super social platforms could be advantageous for any business, brand or professional or any other type of business, professional, etc. who wish to be more prominent on the Internet for both them and their products or services, in front of all the thousands of customers (or possible customers) that are.

This social media tool for advertising along with other functions allows us to make various types of publications and group them according to the specifics of the targeted or intended audience you want to target them.

We can create segmented advertisements with parameters that include:

* City or country of the place of.

* Language.

* Sex.

The status of the marriage.

* Personal preferences, interests, preferences of the user, and so on.

On the other hand those very same strategies that are geared towards monetizing their platforms through promoting companies to use targeted publications, or Ads advertisements, has made it clear that via this social media platform, the tools that we can use to advertise are continuously enhanced.

The success of the acquisition of Instagram at the time was also the perfect opportunity to create advertising advertisements for businesses that are on the visual platform and all via Facebook's Facebook Ads Manager platform itself.

The integration of advertisements through Instagram along with Ads gives us additional options to reach more potential customers and boost the ROI of an ad campaign.

Another trend that has been consolidated on this social media platform is video, and of course, it's an excellent way to present your ads on Facebook Ads.

The company pages will increase your visibility and sales by using the video format used in your advertisements.

Maybe, in light of everything discussed above, despite their desire to promote their business on Facebook however, many small and medium-sized businesses have a lot of doubts about their strategy for advertising and investing.

In the end there are many companies who do not comprehend how to make use of (even from a fundamental point of view) this online marketing tool.

Mega Facebook Ads Guide Everything you should be aware of when advertising on Facebook!

In this instance, I'd be happy to help you comprehend this platform, and also make plans and design your own campaigns for advertising I am here to provide you with most up-to-date information on all modifications that took place up to the year 2019.

Facebook advertising tools

Remember that we have numerous tools on this social media platform. To promote herself, she offers us two.

This is the tools available at present, you can access in your corporate account

Remember that we have numerous tools on this social platform to promote itself, it offers three options:

* Business Manager

It is a website specially created for brands that allows access to their websites to professionals or agencies who manage multiple accounts. They are only able to be assigned an advertising task, without the requirement for a more extensive link, like being administrators of the identical.

The major differences of this tool is that there isn't a direct connection between pages and profiles which means:

It is also extremely beneficial for those who oversee multiple brands, which can help avoid errors or mixing different brands under the same account.

• Ad Manager

It allows you to create and manage ads, campaigns and other advertisements quickly and easily.

In this section, I will be teaching you how to make the most of your advertisements using the Ad Manager. However some of the advice I'll give you can be used for those who use the Power Editor and Business Manager.

This is how the Ads Manager appears as in the year the year 2019. The comment can be made as a result of the fact that it is known that the system is constantly altering its interface.

Through the Ad Manager you are able to manage monitoring, evaluation, and control of your advertising campaigns.

In other words, if we recall that Facebook is the network that has the most users and taking into consideration that this type of advertisement is among the most cost-effective, then conducting an Facebook Ads campaign would make our Internet advertising investment much more lucrative.

In particular, if we design and segment it properly.

Campaign structures are part of Facebook Ads that advertise with ads setting options

In the infographic I will show below, and which was created by the team from FB For Business>>, we can see the design of the campaigns that are part of Facebook Ads.

Because of this structure, it's much easier to manage and optimize our advertising efforts.

Let's take a closer look at this advertisement structure for businesses:

* Campaign

Every campaign has to be based on a single objective of the available 11 (we will provide you with a list in the future) for all of its standard ads.

* Ad set

A campaign could have multiple sets of ads or groups.

However, each set of ads must be defined by a budget bid, schedule, and segmentation of the audience for every one their ads.

* Advertisements

Within every set of advertisements, there are a variety of advertisements.

Each of them has diverse combinations of text, images video, links, and call-to action buttons (but they all share the budget and segmentation of the entire set).

What kinds of advertising objectives and types of ads are available on Facebook Ads?

Facebook has changed some features, and we now have 11 different goals for our campaigns.

* Recognition

These are the goals that you can attract interest to the products or services you provide:

1. Brand recognition

You'll get more exposure for your brand and reach those who are likely to have an interest in your brand.

2. Reach

Increase the number of people you reach through your ads by achieving this kind of objective.

* Take into consideration

If you achieve these goals, you'll be able to attract others' interest in your business and consequently, learn more about it. We can distinguish between:

3. Traffic

* It draws users to a location either on Facebook or offline. Facebook.

Increase the number of qualified visitors (or qualified visitors) to various locations on your Facebook profile or on your website in line with your goals or the importance of each.

4. Interaction

Get more people to interact with your posts. I love those you receive, or the response to the events or offers you've put out.

6. Application Downloads

If you have already developed an application, this is an opportunity to see how you can increase the popularity of the app.

Increase the number of people to sign up to your mobile app, or even within Facebook.

7. Video views

Find more viewers to view the video.

If you're a proponent of video Marketing You could promote your videos using unpublished images such as product launches, stories from customers to boost the recognition of your brand.

8. Generation of customers who could be potential

This will help you draw in prospective customers.

In other words, your company will have a template that allows you to collect and gather information from customers, such as newsletter subscriptions prices, price estimates, and subsequent calls.

* Conversion

By utilizing these goals, you will be encouraging that the individuals who have shown an enthusiasm for your services or products will eventually purchase them:

9. Conversions

Improve conversions on your site.

Increase the number of visitors to your site to ensure that they take particular actions when they visit it.

One of the conversions you could achieve this goal might include:

* Sales

* Downloads for ebooks.

* Newsletter Subscriptions .

* Hire services

This is where you need to utilize an pixel for conversion tracking, to ensure that you are able to evaluate these results.

10. The sales of the catalog of products

In this way, you can create ads that highlight items from your catalog which are targeted at those who might be interested in these products.

11. Visits to business

Encourage people to visit your company.

By deciding to do this, you can advertise the various areas of your company (in the event that you have multiple locations) to increase in the number of customers who visit it.

It's a goal which is centered on attracting customers near to your physical company.

I'll then show you the choices available in the present, so that you can choose which you prefer based on the goals the campaign is aiming for.

How do we segment the target viewers of our ads in Facebook Ads?

After we've selected and chosen an objective, we will be presented with an additional page on which we can select which target audience we'd like to send our ads.

It is vital to be aware of who or what we want to attract through the campaign we're planning to create as if it is shown to someone who does not view it as a pleasing piece of content, we'll be investing our money in a wasteful manner.

This is the reason Facebook Ads allows you to divide the viewers to whom our advertisements will be targeted by various parameters.

Who are we hoping to watch our ads?

We will then look at how we can make an audience segmentation in order to display our ads (if we already have an audience segmentation before, we could select it , instead of creating an entirely new one)

* Custom audiences

Segment the ads that will be shown to those you select based on your own selection criteria.

If you click on the link"Create a personal audience" we will get a pop-up window similar to that one where we can select the kind of audience we would like to build from the various choices that Facebook gives us.

You can define and build an audience for your own through:

* Client file: Use the your own file with your own customer details to identify which of them already have an account on Facebook account, and be able to create an audience that is personalized to your own customers to show your advertisements to. It is possible to import them into the text document or Mailchimp. The process for import is guided and can be quite easy.

Web traffic send your advertisements to people who typically visit your site or other pages on the internet. You can choose the exact URLs that you would like to target your audience and also the duration of time that you will be considered for this option.

* Activity in the app If you've got an application, you could create an inventory of all the users who interact with the application.

* Off-line activities: If there is already a database that contains the details of those who have previously interacted with your

company, you can make use of it to target your advertisements to the people who you have gathered from outside the social media.

* Interactions with Facebook Choose the people who have the highest engagement with your content, and then create a list of the people who have the most interaction. You can choose people who have watched a video or have filled out an application or any of your canvas areas.

* Locations

You can determine the geographic segmentation of your advertisements based on these requirements:

1. First Everyone is here.

2nd people living in this area.

* Third People who have recently visited this area.

* 4th people who travel through this area.

After selecting one of these factors, we will select the provinces, countries cities, states or provinces of the general public from the set of advertisements.

In this case, we'll also have the option of applying exclusion segmentation. In other words, you could exclude certain locations (country an area, a province, or a specific cities).

* Age

You can choose between a minimum the age (13 year olds) and an age of maximum (+65 Years).

* Sex

You can make your ad visible only to males either exclusively for women or to everyone.

* Language

Choose the language of those who are able to view your publication.

* Detailed segmentation

In This Area, You Are able to Segment Your Audience Through:

Demographic data: These are the most important data that are derived from the biographical data that every user has filled in on their profile, including education or work, romantic relationship and political beliefs, etc.

Interests: These segmentation parameters are then created according to the interests or customs that Facebook users typically display in their interactions on Facebook.

This is that they are the categories of pages they are avid fans and the type of publication they most frequently interact with as well as the articles that they are most in contact with in a way, and the ability to discuss activities and entertainment, sports shopping, food and drinks, etc.

Behaviors They are segmentation criteria that focus on activities or behavior that people typically engage in to deal with in their daily lives such as occasions or trips they've taken or participated in.

More categories: Facebook's personal categories.

You may use the alternative to be excluded by any of the criteria listed above.

Connections

Then, you have the option to separate your audience based on the relationship the user or fan has with our page. You can choose from:

1. First Connections to your company's Facebook page.

* 2nd Connections for your application.

* 3rd Connections in conjunction with your event.

In the same way, you may be excluded under these criteria, and mix several criteria simultaneously.

While we decide and set the criteria for our target audience We can view within the column to the right, the real-time estimate Facebook Ads provides of the reach potential of the audience we have selected, along with some indications which will be used as feedback.

The target we have identified and analyzing our community's social media profiles and other platforms, it can be beneficial to collect data that can greatly improve our criteria in the process of segmentation.

Recommendation: we should not attempt to reach out to everyonebecause in the end, we won't reach everyone.

If there isn't an incalculable amount of money to fund our campaigns the most sensible thing to do is to ensure, via segmentation, a potential amount of people who could be reached (about 200 000 people).

It all depends on the nature of the campaign and investment and the budget will be reduced as the budget is established at the next stage.

In other words, if we are obsessed with reaching many people, we may sacrifice some of our segmentation (for lack of a large budget) it could result in a loss of the effectiveness of our campaign and, as we've said previously, may end up showing an ad to people who aren't interested in the person.

Placement of ads in Facebook ads

Once we've defined our target audience The next step to designing our advertising set is to decide the location where our ads are to be placed.

Your ads will be shown at various locations, but you can also choose to select exactly what are displayed.

There are two methods to pick the right location.

1. Automatic places

We leave Facebook with Facebook the selection of the most effective locations for our ads throughout the day.

Our advertisements can be seen in the following locations:

*Facebook (news sections and instant articles, as well as in-stream videos the right-hand column).

* Instagram (news section) and Instagram Stories).

* Audience Network

* Messenger (home and sponsored messages).

2. Edit the locations

By choosing this option, we have complete control over the places where our ads will be placed.

You are able to segment and select in accordance with the following criteria for the areas where your advertisements can be shown:

* By type of device All, phones (1) and the only computer.

* Based on individualization of resources: this choice lets us select different videos or images in the same commercial, based on the location of their display.

* Based on the type of platform such as Facebook (News section (2) Instant articles, and in the column to the right (3)), Instagram (4) (news and stories), Audience Network (native banners, interstitial and in-stream videos, award-winning video) as well as Messenger (incio and messages with sponsored content).

* Advanced options

It is also possible to segment using Wi-Fi or mobile devices in addition to other connections.

How does Facebook calculates the cost of an ads?

The next step in the setup of our collection of Facebook ads is to determine the budget and calendar.

The amount or quantity of each advertisement will be determined by the configuration we create of the various variables that will be explained in the following paragraphs.

* Enter the campaign budget

Budgets can be set up for a long length of time (i.e the campaign) or simply for a daily average.

Keep in mind it is important to remember that your budget has been for the entire set of ads rather than per advertisement.

* Define the period of circulation

You are able to decide if require it to be of the same time frame (start the day, end it along with the time) or if you want it to run continuously.

* Optimization for ad delivery

This is why Facebook is now offering us three major types or types of optimization in relation to the calculation of price of shares in our upcoming announcement.

* Posts that have interaction The advert will be shown to people who are most likely to engage with the post.

* Impressions: They will present the advertisement to the public as many times as they can.

* Single-day reach: they'll show our advertisement up to one time or X times per day.

Price of bid (choose what you'd like to offer)

There are two obvious alternatives, and in the second (Automatic) the bid is then automatically optimized for greater interactions or for more impressions.

The second (Manual) in the second (Manual) establish the prices that these actions will achieve in the auctions.

Important: Depending on the delivery method selected, the cost will be determined by cost per impression (CPI) as well as per click.

* CPM or PPM: cost per 1,000 impressions (CPM) or bid per 1,000 impressions (PPM). A impression is similar to a visual.

This means that we will pay for each 1,000 times that someone is exposed to the ad in all the various places Facebook offers to offer this (news part of computer computer news section of the mobile or cell phone or the right column) however, the publication isn't getting any action or click whatsoever.

CPC, or PPC: This is cost per click (CPC) or cost per Click (PPC).

In this case, we'll be paid for every click on our website.

When does it get being billed?

Based on the goal you have chosen in this case, it is possible to display the time during which you'll be billed. It could be per impression is provided or when the user performs an action within an advertisement (one Click).

Ad Programming

You can choose the particular days or times of the week your ads to show.

Delivery method

This option lets you select between standard or rapid delivery.

It is beneficial to utilize the speedier version to start advertising campaigns that require you to immediately start contacting your intended public quickly.

30 Free Facebook Tools for Businesses

You may consider that Facebook isn't a great social network to make use from and "blow you teeth" due to the frequent changes to its algorithm , which have led to its organic traffic to drop substantially, however, despite this negative view, we should continue placing bets on this social network. The reason for this are due to the fact that it is the second source of social media with the highest web traffic.

The advertisements on Facebook are also an efficient tool for generating sales for any business however, it is vital that we separate the target viewers of our ads so that they be effective and achieve the highest return on investment.

In this instance I've rediscovered a few Facebook instruments that may not be used by everyone, yet that still provide excellent results for any social media plan I've finished them off with a solid collection of a few lesser-known Facebook instruments that are sure to provide plenty to discuss in 2018/2019.

Note: Virtually all of the tools are free, with the one thing is that a few offer trial versions for free and once the trial time is over their functionality will be restricted.

Essential and Free Facebook Tools

1. Audience Insights

If you want to be successful with your plan for success on Facebook it is essential to know individuals who might be interested in either your company or products to be able to identify things like locations, interests, behaviors and so on. in order to be used to enhance your marketing on Facebook.

With Facebook Audience Insight, you are able to build an audience of your very own based upon your interests associated with your brand . You can create various kinds of targeted audiences that you can later develop ads on Facebook Ads.

Find out about the locations of your audience as well as their interests and habits, to create messages that help grow your business.

2. Debugger: Shared Content Debugger

Have you ever had the experience that you've shared an article or webpage in Facebook and the picture you were looking for didn't appear or hasn't provided you with any photos?

This is caused on numerous occasions to the cache of Facebook itself.

Don't be worried, Facebook comes with a tool that can cleanse of Facebook cache and display the photo of your latest article.

Simply type in the URL that causes you trouble under the "Shared Content Debugger" section, and then click Debug.

3. LikeAlyzer

This tool on Facebook is extremely fascinating, as it conducts an analysis within a matter of seconds on our Facebook fan page and informs us in a simple manner what we can do to enhance.

Additionally, you can use these tools that are free to look at other corporate pages on Facebook.

4. Headline Analyzer

We all understand the importance of selecting a quality title for your publication, both to boost SEO and also to get more engagement on Facebook this is the reason why using this tool, you can examine the title you intend to publish in order to ensure that it's optimized for social SEO from the perspective of optics.

5. Sumome

Still don't have a clue about Sumome?

It is among the best free WordPress plugins available because we can utilize it to increase our functionality, gain readers to our Blog as well as to bring subscribers to our Blog, which is just another end of the spectrum however, we can also use it to ensure that our content are more easily shared via Facebook as well as various other Social Networks, both articles and images can be posted across any social media platform with ease.

6. Simply Measured Free

An analysis of the free Facebook fan page

Free report of the company's page on Facebook.

No cost Facebook Insights Analysis

Analyzing the demographics of your users on Facebook and their activities.

A free Facebook competitive analysis

Examine Your Company Facebook page against your competitor's page.

A free analysis of Facebook's content

Free report to analyze the level of optimization for our content that is published on Facebook.

7. Cyfe

This tool will get all your analytics on one dashboard. It is a highly recommended tool.

8. The Week's Fan

This app lets you choose"the "fan that week" and honor your contributions to our Facebook page.

9. Shared Count

One of the most effective tools to analyze and exported in Excel the most popular posts on Social Networks of other blogs that relate to your subject.

It is recommended to access the sitemaps of other blogs and then extract the URLs of all their blogs to study the content using Shared Count.

Tools to study the Facebook competition
Facebook

10. Facebook Barometer

Check if your company's Facebook page has excellent results, or your page is not performing as well as the average of other companies on the Social Network.

The average compares it to a certain number of Fan Pages based on a set amount of fan pages with an amount of followers that are similar to ours. This lets us know:

The percentage of readers that were reached through each issue.

The percentage of people "talking" to us.

The percentage of CTR.

The % of engagement

11. Buzzsumo

A tool that we can easily analyze for free the most popular blog posts from our Blog and similar Blogs.

It's easy to use and within only a few minutes we can get extremely interesting information about publications that have performed well, and we ought to think about adding in our editorial calendar.

12. Karma Fanpage

An essential tool for studying an organization's profile Facebook is a must-have tool to analyze a company's page on Facebook But I'd like to be highlighting the following points:

Analyzing the best and most shady Facebook content.

The most frequently used keyword and hashtags.

The most frequently used websites.

The length of your Facebook post Facebook.

The best days and times to upload.

Fan growth curve.

Another aspect that I admiring about this program is the fact that it lets us to analyze the different Facebook pages of businesses and analyse the performance of your competitors.

13. Ahrefs

This SEO tool is constantly growing, initially it was used to analyse the link on our site.

Today, it's also a useful tool for studying the keywords.

It also serves the ability to track the most popular content on Facebook in that particular domain.

To do this , you just need to enter the domain, and then within the pages section you will have to select the best results and content on Facebook from the highest to the lowest.

14. Facebook Insight

Facebook is home to its own analysis of competition, and we can integrate the pages of our principal competitors.

To accomplish this, visit Analytics, then select publications and then go to the Featured publication section on your pages that are under observation.

We will be able to see the most recent posts you have posted and your engagement level so that we can figure out which content is most effective for you.

15. OctoSuite

OctoSuite is a Facebook tool Facebook I love as it lets me conduct an analysis of the competitor's Facebook strategy.

While it's a pay application however, the amount of data you can get is useful, such as:

* I enjoy the images as well as the videos and links that contain more.

* The most current content.

* The most popular content on the Fan Page of the competition.

Tools for creating contests on Facebook

16. Easy Promos

Easy Promos is one of the most popular tools available to create contests through Facebook.

There are many ways to conduct contests, such as:

Video contests

Photo contests

Text contests

Etc.

17. Cool tabs

Additionally, it is an excellent tool for analytics on Facebook (as we'll see in the future) by using Cool Tabs we are also able to run raffles and contests through Facebook.

Contests can be conducted three different ways:

Photo contests

Video contests

Text contests.

18. Time Line contest on Facebook using the Agora Pulse

Contests that are completely free to enter via Facebook's Time Line. Facebook Time Line.

Does Facebook allow me to run contests directly through my Timeline?

Yes! Since July 27, 2013,, you can organize Contests using your Timeline without the use of third-party apps.

Tools to keep track of Facebook

Monitoring social media for negative and positive reviews about the brand is among the most important tasks of a community manager.

In order to accomplish this, we may use various tools like:

19. Brand24

Brand24 is a monitoring app which will let us track the frequency they feature our company on Facebook in the course of the course of time.

Additionally, it lets us filter our search by:

* Sentiment

* Influence of those who refer to us.

20. Xovi

The Xovi SEO tool, however it includes a comprehensive section on social media.

There are many capabilities that Xovi enables us to perform one of them is to look over the comments made by users on Facebook and apply various filters.

For example, we could filter negative terms, and by doing this, we can analyze possible negative reviews about our brand and respond as needed.

The tools to control Facebook

21. HootSuite

The most effective tool for managing all of our Facebook accounts. If we are able to master it correctly, we can observe how it helps us to save between 2 and three hours each week.

Hootsuite is the most widely used tool to schedule and manage your posts on #RedesSociales.> quote = the most commonly used tool to manage and plan your posts in #RedesSociales.>

22. Buffer

Buffer lets you post your content at the time of the day when your audience is most active. This means that when you will get the greatest outcomes.

You can make lists of programming which will make it easier to save time you would normally devote making manual posts on Facebook.

23. Facebook Publishing Tool

We've seen many tools to program content on Facebook but the one I like the best can be found in Facebook's very own tool for publishing.

When you post it offers you the possibility of programming your content on your own. If you wish to view all the publications are pending to be published You will need to set up publishing tools and choose scheduled publications.

Facebook analytics tools

Analytics is an essential component of any online company.

The analysis of what is being done and what strategies work best or do not is crucial to determine if the social media strategy is working or not.

A few of the tools for analysis used by Facebook that we could use include:

24. Facebook Insight

The ultimate Facebook tools for analytics is Facebook Insight.

If you're a community manager who manages many Facebook accounts for clients one of your duties is to create various reports to assess the results of the activities you've carried out.

To accomplish this, you have familiar with this no-cost Facebook tool and its analytic section, which will enable us to learn:

What publications and magazines are gaining reach.

* What type of content is most effective.

25. Google Analytics

One of the main goals we typically set when establishing the social strategy is to increase visitors to our site.

Therefore, to know whether the actions we are doing are working, we shouldn't be able to test it.

To do this, we will utilize Google Analytics and will examine which social networks receives more visits and how they contribute to the accomplishment of our goals.

26. Metricool

Metricool is the perfect tool for both programming content for Facebook as well as its social network analytics feature.

We can get together:

* The growth in our fan Page

* The remaining followers

* The pages that function best on our site.

Alongside knowing what are the post that have the most popularity in Facebook we can sort them by:

* Engagement (reactions or comments, as well as shares)

* Clicks

* Impressions

* Scope

27. Cool tabs

Cool Tabs is another tool for Facebook which will give us some interesting statistics including:

* The averagepercentage of people we can reach via our publications.

* The number of users we can reach through organically.

* A new degree of involvement.

* CTR for our publications.

It also permits us to see the stats of each publication and also apply different filters.

The reality is that it is an extremely comprehensive tool that has to be taken into consideration.

28. Superb Facebook Analytics

Find out the effectiveness of your posts on Facebook as well as some other information related to them are very interesting like for example the CTR or the percent of spam.

Tools to advertise on Facebook

29. Ad Express

An application that allows users to examine the effectiveness of paid advertisements on Facebook and then create reports that are easy to comprehend by the user that is, it provides us with a variety of important and relevant information in a no-cost report that is easy to understand.

It's certainly a valuable tool for analyzing the effectiveness of your Facebook ads..

30. Creative hub

The Creative Hub is one of the less well-known Facebook tool that lets you to test the way your ads will appear on Facebook.

The most important thing about this app is that it gives you the dimensions that are recommended for each kind of ad on Facebook.

31. Cover Tool for Compliance

If the text is more than 20 percent of the image, Facebook won't allow you to incorporate it into paid advertisements right on Facebook.

Slogans, logos and emblems.

Images that are clearly altered to include text within the product in order to circumvent the rules.

32. Reviewing the text on the Facebook image

Furthermore, Facebook also has its own tool that analyzes the content of ads and provide informative information regarding the content of the advertisement and its text.

33. Pixel Caffeine

If you're determined to advertise on Facebook Ads, you must include the Facebook Pixel on your website whether you want it or not.

If you don't want to make your life more complicated by directly inserting the code on your site, there are a variety of WordPress plugins that can make life easier.

34. Facebook Pixel Helper

Okay, we have the Facebook Pixel installed However, have we implemented it correctly?

Through this Chrome extension, we are able to know.

In general, it is best to make sure to ensure that the "thank to you" pages have the right events properly set up and will don't give anyone a fright later.

How to Create An Effective Social Media Marketing Strategy For Your Business or Company? Plus, examples

How can you design an effective social media marketing strategy?

Being able to craft an expertly designed social media strategy is an extremely valuable addition to the digital Marketing strategy employed by any modern business. In this article we've prepared an extensive tutorial step by procedure, with illustrations.

There are a lot of companies which, even though they have an impressive presence in social media, don't really know why or the reason behind how they operate. This is typically due to the lack of an adequate social media strategy as part of their business plans and their online communications.

What is the definition of a social media marketing social media strategy?

The Social Media plan is the organizing, planning, and adjusting of various social media we have within our reach to build an online channel of communication that we can use with our users, with the aim of achieving the goals our company requires and where the user is always situated in the middle.

What is the reason your company should be properly planned?

The explosive growth of social media is the response to the need of users to stay connected with one another.

Sharing stories, experiences, and views with people from different backgrounds is a part that social nature, which has been integrated into people's everyday lives.

These channels of communication are a great option for companies to use to create a new channel for their marketing strategies. These channels, when properly utilized and managed by an experienced Community Manager can help them establish an immediate connection with prospective and current customers.

The number of social networks users grow year on year. The new, hyperconnected generation prefers to use social media and makes enterprises more open.

What factors should we take into consideration when developing a social media strategy?

How do you create a plan for marketing on social media?

Making a social media-based marketing strategy isn't an easy job. However, in general those who don't engage in social media might think it's only to select the platform on which you'll have a presence and then dedicate yourself to publishing content you think is fascinating. In reality, this is much more meticulous and thorough work.

Similar to any other offline or online program Social media plans is designed in a variety of parts which are vital and complement to one another and in which you have to put in the most effort to build them.

Before you begin to develop the strategy, you should have all the information you can about the company to which you'll develop the complete plan (in order to be successful with your recommendations).

Step one: Analyzing and briefing: crucial questions to be answered

Before beginning to create the section, start by examining the information you have on your possession and answering a number of questions that define the features of the company and form the base of the entire procedure.

A list of questions to ask before we design the social media strategy (SWOT analysis)

Focusing on the item or service

1. What we offer Description of the items or services we offer in our company, indicating the primary and related ones.

2. Where can we sell it? Geographical coverage

3. Do you have your own website? Are you selling online? What have you done in the digital realm?

4. Are you able to determine if it is a seasonal service? When is the peak demand?

5. What is the present market conditions?

6. What is our unique value proposition and how do we differentiate ourselves from the rest of the market.

Focusing on the client or audience

1. Who do we sell to? We will be selling to. Please identify each of them and the characteristics.

2. Identify your target audience in social networks.

3. What are the needs we can meet by offering our product or service? We might offer different offerings for each of our target audiences.

4. How do your online clients behave? Do they appear to be Internet users? Do they have access to networks?

5. What are the worries or challenges that clients may be facing? It is possible to look

through blogs, forums, on specific websites... in order to learn what they are thinking about the services you provide.

6. Customer languages.

7. Which countries do our customers originate from? Local, national, foreigners ...

In the direction of the business or the company

The size of the company and resources available.

What have we seen so far on the internet?

We are present on social media, but not sure? As...

What actions have been implemented?

Do you mention our work on the social networks? forums, blogs, networks, ...?

What are the opinions of others about us Does it sound either positive or negativ?

Conclusion

This guide will teach you a number of techniques that you probably didn't know about previously. There's a reason these techniques aren't discussed. They're not well-known. Some people who earn a living by in educating others on how to quickly become instant online millionaires overnight by doing internet marketing aren't keen on you learning about these methods.

They don't want you to learn the work required. They don't want you to realize that there's a better method. They don't want you to be aware of the possibility of being able to reduce your chances of success simply by reverse engineering other people's success. They don't want you to realize that you may be able to use the strengths of your competitors to complete the due diligence you need to do for yourself.

They want to keep your in the dark about the whole thing. Why would they do this? They would like you to believe that if you publish highly sought-after content, people likely to appear on your website. They would like you to keep coming back to them for guidance. They're not really trying to provide you with

183

the complete foundation you need to can start your journey.

Please be aware that I'm providing you with the complete structure. You must continue to test, tweak and modify what you're doing to make your life better. This will allow you to refine your results, and ultimately achieve your ultimate success. In the case of online content that is viral, it really is all about identifying what works , and then building upon it.

If you believe this it is a good idea to be successful. But if you think that you just need to steal other people's work and spend a small amount of time and effort in syndicating the content, you won't be very successful. Be aware that, ultimately everything boils down to how much value you bring to the lives of others.

The bottom line is. If you apply the suggestions and tips that I've included in this guide, with a positive outlook in your mind, you're bound be doing well. I would like nothing more than the greatest success.